Advance Praise for

Famous Faces Decoded

MEDIA PUNDITRY & PROGRAMMING

There's no one I would trust more to READ MY LIPS, not to mention my eyes, my eyebrows and everything else on my face than Dan Hill. He's the guy I go to when I need famous faces analyzed for one of my pieces, when I need someone to tell me which politician was lying during a debate. I'd be lying (and Dan would catch me) if I said Dan Hill isn't the best facial coder out there.

Jeanne Moos, CNN

I had the good fortune to interview Dan Hill a few years ago at the U.S. Open Tennis Championships in New York. Dan's an avid tennis fan, and I'm a lifelong player and lover of the game. So I was deeply interested in his study of facial coding and how it applies to tennis players. I have watched an extraordinary amount of matches over the years, and among the great gifts of my favorite sport is this: that for a couple of hours you can watch and study two supreme athletes to see not only the strategies, tactics, physical and mental capabilities they possess, but also see the primal power of their emotions.

Dan sees a lot more than most: sadness, anxiety, disgust, anger, fear, contempt. There are many different ways to be a tennis champion, and in the course of a match there are many facial cues to read and interpret—to understand better the process of champions, and sometimes their downfall. Dan Hill offers fascinating insights into the mind, heart, strengths and weaknesses of all manner of famous people: in politics, Hollywood, and for people like me, Center Court at Wimbledon. His work is illuminating, and you should know that as I write this, I'm smiling.

Mary Carillo, Tennis Channel, NBC Sports, HBO Sports

I love this book! Famous Faces Decoded *is a perfect reduction of Dan Hill's incredible facial coding abilities. In my competitive entertainment world, which is so personality driven, Hill's latest work is highly useful and relevant.*

Benjamin Ringe, CEO and Executive Producer of B.Bold Content Studios LLC

ACADEMIA

A lively and creative, non-academic—but highly-informed and knowledgeable—discussion of how to read faces that many of us could learn a lot from—so long as we remember that no approach to reading people is perfect.

John D. Mayer, author of *Personal Intelligence: The Power of Personality and How It Shapes Our Lives*

Whether you find yourself in the boardroom or the living room, it pays to perceive others' faces well. With two decades of experience, Dan Hill teaches us in Famous Faces Decoded *how to apply the science of facial coding to our friends, colleagues, strangers and, yes, those famous celebrities around the globe. If you want to read a truly practical book, you've found it.*

Matthew Hertenstein, Ph.D., Associate Professor of Psychology at DePauw University and author of *The Tell: The Little Clues That Reveal Big Truths about Who We Are*

Dan Hill's book provides an entertaining and palatable guide to decoding the faces that populate our daily lives.

Sam Gosling, Ph.D., Associate Professor of Psychology at the University of Texas at Austin and author of *Snoop: What Your Stuff Says about You*

PERSONAL LIFE

Absolutely fascinating! Every page of Famous Faces Decoded *will mesmerize you. The practical applications of this compelling book are endless and you won't be able to put it down.*

Drs. Les & Leslie Parrott, *New York Times* bestselling authors of *Saving Your Marriage Before It Starts*

Dan has the superhero skills everybody wishes they had—he reads people through their facial expressions. I asked him to teach a room full of matchmakers and relationship experts the secrets to facial coding. He rocked the room and every single person left wanting more. In the love profession, Dan's knowledge and skill set is crucial, so this book is a must read for anyone who wants to connect and understand others.

Lisa Clampitt, LMSW, CMM President and Founder Lisa Clampitt Matchmaking & Matchmaking Institute

GENERAL BUSINESS

Can you read the emotions on another person's face? Dan Hill sure can. Even better, he can teach you to do the same. In his terrific new book, Hill uses celebrity faces to help us improve our ability to identify and recognize other people's emotional states. FAMOUS FACES DECODED is a valuable primer on understanding emotions, the rare book that manages to be both entertaining and enlightening—often on the same page.

Daniel H. Pink, author of *WHEN* and *DRIVE*

In Famous Faces Decoded, *Hill shows the way to benefit from a spontaneous, real-life feedback loop as to what others in your life are feeling, thanks to what their faces reveal. Positive or negative emotions are incorrect labels, as Hill shows us. Instead the key is to understand how any emotion, from happiness to fear, can offer both reliable information about what motivates the other party and the likely behavior to expect. Armed with that knowledge, you can achieve better rapport and a better outcome for all involved.*

**Jon Gordon, best-selling author of
*The Power of Positive Leadership***

LEADERSHIP & MANAGEMENT

Recent research on leadership has found that the ability to recognize and understand emotions are among the best predictors of successful leaders. Rarely, however, are these emotional intelligence skills taught in business schools. Dan Hill presents a unique and highly entertaining roadmap to these skills. I highly recommend Famous Faces Decoded *as a way to improve your ability to read emotions in other people's faces. It's a great step towards increasing your own emotional intelligence.*

**Steven Stein, Ph.D., CEO of MHS Assessments, author of
The EQ Leader and coauthor of *The EQ Edge***

This is an extremely fascinating book on assessing the personality and emotional intelligence of people by observing their facial cues. The book uses famous faces to illustrate the technique, which is highly applicable to business in selecting people for jobs or promotions or in people's personal relationships. You will certainly enjoy this book. It makes a real contribution to our understanding of human behaviour and is a great read.

**Professor Sir Cary Cooper, ALLIANCE Manchester Business
School, University of Manchester, England**

SALES PROSPECTS & CUSTOMERS

In Famous Faces Decoded, *you will learn to understand what other people are emoting, especially when their words don't match their facial expression, a critical tool for improving your emotional intelligence. More importantly, you will learn even more about yourself and the signals that you are giving others.*

Anthony Iannarino, bestselling author of *The Lost Art of Closing: Winning the 10 Commitments That Drive Sales*

With facial coding, Dan Hill again gives us another tool to help us read people and situations more clearly. Following his lead, you will add to your ability to interpret the words people say, but may or may not always mean.

Linda Richardson, founder of Richardson and author of *Changing the Sales Conversation*

This book is a must-read—and must-absorb!—for all those who embrace the Experience Economy. It will enable you to truly understand what your customers feel throughout your experience, enabling frontline workers as well as managers to more personally engage guests and enhance the emotional experience you design, create, and stage. Moreover, recognize that in the Experience Economy work is theatre, so experience staging itself is emotional labor. Famous Faces Decoded *will enable employees to not only act well, but act authentically.*

B. Joseph Pine II, coauthor of *The Experience Economy* and *Authenticity: What Consumers Really Want*

HIRING & PERSONNEL

Executive interviews are different from other interviews—they need to be, there's more at stake. Research shows that companies with great executive talent significantly outperform their competitors in revenue and EBITDA growth. The tactics and strategies in Famous Faces Decoded: A Guidebook for Reading Others, *will light your path to decoding facial expressions and separating fact from fiction. You'll set the world on fire where others get burned. Steeped in Hill's wry humor and unabashed candor, this book will quickly become your secret weapon!*

David Perry, Managing Partner of Perry-Martel Int'l, author of *Executive Recruiting for Dummies* and *Hiring Greatness: How to Hire Your Dream Team and Crush the Competition*

HIRING & PERSONNEL (CONTINUED)

In running Philadelphia's most successful radio station for years, you get attuned to reading our on-air personalities carefully. They must be able to connect with the listeners. Dan has been a consultant with our radio station for years—so I'm familiar with his expertise in facial coding and his analytical abilities. Using those unique talents to analyze celebrities makes for a fascinating read!

Jerry Lee, Chairman of WBEB MORE-FM and President of the Jerry Lee Foundation

LAWYERS & POLICE

I don't think anyone could find a person who has greater insight in evaluating experts' sincerity and potential jurors than Dan Hill. To obtain objective insights into feelings is priceless. His ability to assist in jury selection in important cases cannot be measured. Dan has the ability to see the true reactions. More importantly, he is one of the kindest and nicest human beings anyone could ever meet.

Thomas V. Girardi, Trial Lawyer Hall of Fame inductee, former President of the International Academy of Trial Lawyers, and the lead attorney in winning a settlement in the famous *Erin Brockovich* case

For the next step in your "emotional intelligence" education, Famous Faces Decoded helps you recognize the emotions of the people you encounter. Dan deftly takes us through celebrity faces in order to guide us in reading the emotions of those we encounter in our own lives. He then takes us a step further, postulating on the WHY of each emotion to powerfully aid us in evaluating the true character of those we seek to understand.

Tanna Moore, MERITAS President & CEO

Police officers would be sorely remiss to overlook this book. It contains insights into decoding facial expression that, when used properly, relay so much more about people's emotions than what their words convey.

Dr. Renée J. Mitchell, Sacramento Police Department Sargent, President of the American Society of Evidence-Based Policing

CONSULTANTS

The intersection of soft and hard science is a messy place. Many social scientists get lost in reductionist, methodology-heavy approaches; others stay in the pop psychology lane. Both are unsatisfying to the bulk of people who just want to learn something valid and practical. Dan Hill delivers on both, and on a fascinating issue: how can you tell what other people are thinking and feeling? In Famous Faces Decoded, he reveals hard research into this issue—yet writes it in real, colloquial English. What are the most common emotions? How can you spot them? Even more importantly, how do they relate to each other—and what do they mean? This is terrific! By using well-known celebrity examples, Hill brings solid scientific insight to the living room reading table. Read for fun, while learning insights for everyday use.

Charles H. Green, founder and CEO of Trusted Advisor Associates and coauthor of *The Trusted Advisor*

SPORTS

Dan's a good guy with real insights. In figuring out how best to prepare and keep your players focused on shutting other teams down, every opportunity to know who you're going to war with is huge. This book does that. It gives you an understanding of people you can build on.

Tubby Smith, one of only five NCAA men's basketball head coaches to win 365 games in 15 seasons or less

Who would have thought that Dan Hill's facial profiling would assist in winning Olympic medals in the sport of diving, but that is just what happened at the 2016 Rio Olympic Games! Dan worked closely with me at the U.S. Olympic Trials for Diving in Indianapolis. His profiling of some of my elite athletes and coaches, followed by his great feedback in relation to their emotions under pressure, was insightful and put to good use. The result—four Olympic medalists! Thank you, Dan, and thank you for this fantastic new book that will assist me in taking coaches and athletes to another level in diving.

Steve Foley, High Performance Director USA Diving 2009–2017

In Famous Faces Decoded, *Dan Hill provides us with an essential tool to accurately read people's emotions and situations. Coaches and leaders in all walks of life will benefit greatly from his wisdom. We now have an effective way to immediately move people forward.*

TJ Kostecky, Men's Soccer Coach, LIU, Brooklyn

famous
faces
DECODED

*A Guidebook
for Reading Others*

Dan  Hill

Sensory Logic Books
www.SensoryLogic.com

1509 Marshall Street, N. E. Suite 400
Minneapolis, MN 55413, USA

Publisher's Cataloging-In-Publication Data
(Prepared by The Donohue Group, Inc.)

Names: Hill, Dan, 1959-
Title: Famous faces decoded : a guidebook for reading others / Dan Hill.
Description: Minneapolis, MN : Sensory Logic Books, [2018] | Includes bibliographical references and index.
Identifiers: ISBN 9780999741603
Subjects: LCSH: Facial expression. | Emotions. | Personality. | Celebrities.
Classification: LCC BF592.F33 H55 2018 | DDC 153.69--dc23

Printed in the United States of America

LCCN 2018903981

Photo Credit: Jack-o'-lantern photo taken October 26, 2010 by Toyah (Public Domain-author's choice). https://commons.wikimedia.org/wiki/File:

Book cover by *the* Book Designers
Book's interior design and illustrations by Karen Bernthal

*It is only shallow people who do not judge
by appearances. The true mystery of the world
is the visible, not the invisible.*

– Oscar Wilde

By the age of 50, a man has the face he deserves.

– George Orwell

*Fame simply means millions of people have
the wrong idea of who you are.*

– Erica Jong

CONTENTS

Introduction

One of the Biggest Hiring Mistakes Ever

It's 1998 and the San Diego Chargers' brain trust has made what it considers to be a smart bet. Three miserable seasons removed from playing in Super Bowl XXIX, the Chargers have traded three draft picks and two current players to another team to secure the second overall pick in the upcoming NFL draft. Their trade leaves the Chargers sitting pretty because almost every football expert agrees that in this year's draft, there are two prospects destined to be future star quarterbacks.

One of those quarterbacks will fulfill that destiny. Now retired, he awaits induction into pro football's Hall of Fame. The other will flame out and eventually go to prison. Which one will the Chargers end up with, and even more importantly for the purpose of this story: which quarterback does the organization think it wants, and why?

In 1998 the team with the first pick of these two "sure winners" is the Indianapolis Colts. Half of the Colts' inner circle favors Ryan Leaf, figuring Leaf has a stronger throwing arm and more upside. The other half favors Peyton Manning because he's "NFL-ready" and more mature.

Fortunately for the Chargers (or so they believe), Leaf prefers to play in San Diego given its great climate and more laid-back lifestyle. When Leaf blows off his pre-draft interview with the Colts, enraging their coach, that maneuver tips the Colts' choice to Manning.[1]

The Chargers are now free to select Leaf and relish their good luck. They don't see Leaf's maturity as a potential issue. Focused instead on Leaf's physical prowess, the Chargers also don't worry that the 20 pounds the guy has recently gained might indicate a suspect work ethic.

What happens next? Leaf is awarded a $31 million, four-year contract that includes the biggest signing bonus ever paid at that time to a rookie, and he rises to the occasion by *fumbling* the first snap of his regular-season career. Things go downhill from there. Leaf's third game features four fumbles, two interceptions, and only one out of 15 passes completed for a total of four yards. In short, Leaf's rookie season becomes, in the words of Chargers' safety Rodney Harrison, "A nightmare you can't even imagine."

After Leaf wins the final pre-season game in 2000, *Sports Illustrated* puts the quarterback on its cover with the headline "Back from the Brink." Hardly. In three years with San Diego, Leaf will post just four wins as a starter. That's over $7.75 million per victory. In the future, an episode of *NFL Top 10* will label Leaf the number one draft bust in the league's history. Even worse, NBC Sports analyst Michael Ventre will name Leaf "the biggest bust in the history of professional sports."

Now you could blame the Chargers' leadership for being dunderheads, but the truth is these kinds of mistakes take place all the time. For example, in 2014 the Cleveland Browns wasted a first-round draft choice on Johnny Manziel, a party boy soon out of the NFL. Beyond the gridiron, half of all new business hires, from CEOs on down through the ranks, fail within 18 months.[2] Romantic relationships likewise fail at an alarming rate, explaining why the most-read story in *The New York Times* in 2016 was "Why You Will Marry the Wrong Person."

The initial point of Leaf's story is to wonder, why would *any* team consider picking him? The overall point is to recognize that everyone misses helpful clues. While there's no foolproof method for successfully evaluating people and situations, the facial coding tool covered in this book will certainly improve your odds.

Overcoming Limitations

Given the money involved and the rigor with which NFL teams approach the draft, you may rightly wonder: how do blunders like picking Leaf and Manziel persist? What's the underlying problem? The answer is that our preconceptions get in the way of noticing what's literally happening before our eyes. As for a solution, actions really do speak louder than words and among the most frequently *overlooked* actions are facial muscle movements, subtle, but full of value.

> **"***Jeff Foster, who runs the NFL's scouting combine, hired Hill in 2011 to evaluate top prospects. He said Hill had a 'master gift' for uncovering a football player's emotional DNA.* **"**
>
> — Excerpt from a front-page story in *The New York Times*[3] about my consulting work both in professional and NCAA Division 1 sports

Just as physical skills can be carefully gauged in settings like the NFL Combine—a week-long event where college players perform physical tests and sit down for interviews with general managers, coaches, and scouts—the same is true for emotional assessments. Gaining a sense of what in the NFL is referred to as "character" can be better handled than it is now in the NFL, and more broadly, by using facial coding. What is this tool? Unlike *face* recognition[4] based on scanning facial *features*, facial coding is *emotion* recognition based on facial *muscle activity*. That activity reveals people's current emotions and, over time, suggests their signature expressions and behavioral tendencies.

Emotions matter, and the most tangible way to read them is in people's faces. How good are we at recognizing feelings? In *Emotional Intelligence 2.0*, the authors state that only 36% of us accurately identify our own emotions while they're happening due to limited self-awareness.[5]

That 36% score for emotion recognition is almost identical to my results for this book. Here is how I proceeded. Ordinary people (hereafter referred to as "voters") were asked to choose, from memory, the top two characteristic emotions that most distinguish *other* people, namely the celebrities I analyzed for *Famous Faces Decoded*. Given eight options, voters chose the top two emotions correctly for each celebrity only about a third of the time (in the proper *first*, then *second most characteristic* order). How did I judge accuracy? By using facial coding to learn which two emotions, per celebrity, proved to be most above-average by amount across a sample of 173 celebrities. No doubt: voters struggled. Even after I decided to allow voters' top two choices to qualify as correct *regardless* of first or second place order, their accuracy level only climbs to 54%.

Being correct only half the time is essentially mere chance: a coin flip. Why weren't the voters I surveyed more on target? What hinders better emotional recognition is threefold in nature.

There is, again, the already mentioned issue of preconceptions. Case in point: like the Chargers' leadership, the Colts' owner Jim Irsay swears by the idea that in the NFL "It's all about the freaking talent." Had Leaf not blown off his interview with their coach, it's altogether possible Leaf could have joined the Colts instead. Next, there's human nature and our tendency to believe lip-service affirmations, versus visual clues to the contrary. We want things to be rosy, so we don't always look closer. Third, without a known method to follow, our visual instincts won't get sharpened.

How to Reliably Read People and Situations

Sherlock Holmes said it best when he remarked: "I have trained myself to notice what I see." Facial coding doesn't mean you have to go find information. It's already there; you just have to recognize it. This great tool originated with Charles Darwin, who was way ahead of his era as the first scientist to take emotions seriously.[7] From his studies, Darwin observed that there are three reasons why the face adroitly reflects and communicates our feelings:

- First is the *universality* of expressions. Yes, the intensity and duration of people's facial expressions may vary by culture, but the basic facial muscle activity by which emotions get conveyed doesn't change by gender, race, or ethnicity.[8]

- Second is the *spontaneity* of expressions. The face is the only place in the body where the muscles either attach just to facial tissue (such as the muscle surrounding the eyes or lips) or to a single bone and facial tissue. Other muscles in our bodies connect bone-to-bone.

- Third is the *abundance* of expressions. People have more facial muscles than any other species on earth, providing a rich signal system. Over 40 structurally and functionally autonomous muscles play a role in our facial expressions.

Almost a hundred years after Darwin published his book, *The Expression of the Emotions in Man and Animals* (1872), Paul Ekman and colleague Wally Freisen at the University of California, San Francisco, set to work on turning the tool into a methodology. The result was the Facial Action Coding System (FACS),[9] completed in 1978 and updated in 2002. In essence, FACS maps which specific facial muscle movements correspond to one or more of the seven core emotions FACS is capable of capturing. The overwhelming majority of academic experts on emotions support the tenets of Ekman's work,[10] and in 2009 *Time* magazine named him as one of the world's 100 Most Influential People.

The 23 facial muscle movements that reveal people's emotional reactions occur in the following parts of the face:

- 8 movements are located in the upper face: they involve the eyes, eyebrows, and nose;

- 15 moments are located in the lower face: they involve the cheeks, mouth, chin, and jaw.

Along the way, facial coding has become part of popular culture. The tool was cited in depth in Malcolm Gladwell's best-seller *Blink: The Power of Thinking Without Thinking* (2005).[11] It provided the basis for Fox's prime-time hit TV series *Lie to Me* (2009–2011), and guided Pixar's wildly successful movie *Inside Out* (2015).

Facial coding is also entering the mainstream of corporate America. A tech start-up called Emotient was at work on automating facial coding when sold to Apple in 2014. Facebook, Google, and Microsoft are all likewise pursuing the automation of facial coding.[12] The software isn't where it needs to be yet, but automated facial coding will continue to improve (and now that major companies are involved, probably quite rapidly). As of my writing this book, the leading software remains, most likely, in the range of only about 60–70% accurate.[13] So for now, at least, your best bet for quality remains knowledgeable, experienced manual facial coders (like myself), people who can attain accuracy levels of 90% or higher.[14] Therefore, this book showcases the output for celebrities manually coded in order to give you the most reliable results possible.

Why You Should Care

Have you ever been in an ambiguous situation? Say a meeting with your boss where not all the cards are on the table. Or a first date where you find the other party seemingly inscrutable. Then, according to a UCLA professor's study that focused on three basic modes of communication, merely seven percent of the essential communication comes from words. The face and the voice deliver the rest, with the face delivering the lion's share: 55%.[15]

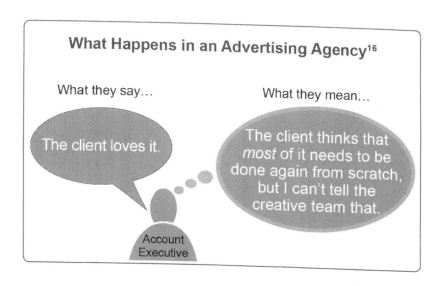

In short, don't focus so much on words—*watch* closely, instead. There's plenty to learn. Unlike IQ, all of us have the ability to improve our emotional intelligence, our EQ, and that's good news. More emotionally intelligent people enjoy better interpersonal relations.[17] To do well in both your professional and personal life, you need a spontaneous, real-time feedback loop you can count on: the information people's faces reveal. Perceiving emotions accurately is in itself an essential skill. Moreover, it opens the door to more complex skills, like using emotions to faciliate thought, social awareness, and stronger rapport with others.

Do I use facial coding in my daily life? Absolutely. I would be crazy not to do so, considering that in tandem with EQ, it offers a great opportunity for improving interactions with others—and therefore outcomes.

The hottest new fields under the umbrella of emotional intelligence are social and personal intelligences, with the latter directly relevant to this book. Clearer, more productive communication arises from an enhanced ability to recognize the consequences of what we say and do, as well as better anticipate the behavior of the people with whom we're interacting. A greater recognition of their emotions, motives, and personalities is crucial to reducing friction and gaining more acceptance from others.

In business, using a combination of facial coding and EQ, I've closed sales by reading prospects. When one person's lower lip stiffened in anger, signaling that I was trying too hard to get her to change her practice, I softened my approach. In another case, when the decision-maker's eyebrows were no longer knitted together, signaling focus, I returned to what had most intrigued him earlier in my presentation and regained momentum.

Off the job, I also use a combination of facial coding and EQ to assess the emotions, authenticity, and personality of people on the nightly news, in TV commercials, and in the countless movies I watch. However, I keep my wife trusting me by *never* telling others what she might be feeling, even when egged on by friends to do so as a "trick" at some dinner party. Now, if only somebody was still willing to sit down and play poker with me.

What You Will (and Won't) Find Here

Famous Faces Decoded is structured around facial coding's seven core emotions and how they organize themselves, according to whether—for the person feeling them—they involve approach or avoidance behavior, and if they point to being dominant or submissive when interacting with others.[18] The size of each emotion's name in the accompanying chart indicates its frequency across my 173-person celebrity sample.[19] Some emotions, like happiness, occur much more often than does an emotion like disgust, and are correspondingly shown in larger type.

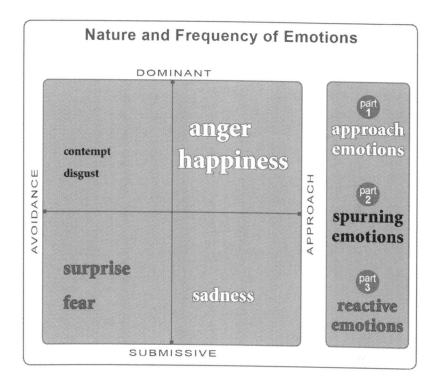

The three approach emotions of anger, happiness, and sadness get handled first. Then I tackle the spurning emotions of contempt and disgust, followed by the reactive emotions of surprise and fear. After you're done reading *Famous Faces Decoded*, you can go on-line at <https://sensory-logic.com/quiz> to take a short, simple quiz that will test your newfound abilities to idenify the expressions of others. For the quiz, photos of the model who appears in this book will again be shown. Should you want to study specific facial expressions of individuals I've analyzed, you can also go on-line to <https://sensorylogic.com/famousfaces> and enter the password "CelebImages" to see a select number of celebity examples.

Also note that because happiness qualifies as the only clearly "positive" emotion of the seven core emotions, I explore it more elaborately. In my facial coding work, I distinguish between four, ever-weaker levels of happiness: joy, pleasure, satisfaction, and acceptance. But to simplify matters for the people who voted on the celebrities' distinguishing, characteristic emotions, I divided happiness into just two categories:

- What I'm calling strong *happiness* is denoted by having *asterisks* around that term in the *voted* results. In regards to the facial coding results, which I call the *actual* results, asterisks adjoin the top two levels of happiness: *joy* and *pleasure*.

- What I'm calling mild happiness appears without asterisks in the voted results. In the facial coding, actual results, that outcome equates to the lower two levels of happiness: satisfaction and acceptance.

For a mock example of a celebrity's emotional profile, let's assume the voters believed Celebrity "X" favors big, intense smiles. So asterisks appear around *happiness* in the voted results. Then because the facial coding confirmed the voters' collective judgment that strong happiness is commonly shown by this celebrity, the actual results specify the level of happiness, which in this case is *pleasure* with asterisks included. Meanwhile, what I'm calling *rare* refers to the celebrity's facially coded, least common, least characteristic emotion, as compared to the other celebrities in my 173-person sample.

Celebrity "X"

Voted

happiness
surprise

Actual

pleasure
sadness

Rare

fear

Other special features in *Famous Faces Decoded* include two sets of Flash Portraits—emotional profiles that compare and contrast celebrities—plus an epilogue on ways to spot lying. The heart of this book, however, remains the seven, emotion-focused chapters. They're structured around each particular emotion's meaning, looks, and likely causes, along with four forms of each emotion and the celebrities who show each form most often. (A separate, companion book, *Decoding Faces*, explores how those four forms may apply in your own life, including advice for how you might best respond when you see a given look from somebody at work or in your off-hours.)

Becoming fluent in what emotions mean and in their likely causes will boost your emotional literacy, and serves as an easy, first level. Learning how each emotion shows on people's faces is the second level. Applying my forms of expression per emotion is the advanced, third level.

With this content, you can gain the inside track on understanding the true, emotional reactions of people, often beyond what they either don't consciously know or won't say. Every emotion has its own nuances and implications for likely future behavior. Discriminate between emotions and you can use that observed information wisely. To describe another person's feelings as simply "negative", for instance, is as inadequate as saying an army now marching in retreat has merely changed its direction. You can do better, and this book aims to help you get there.

part **1** one

emotions

Anger

Pushing Ahead

What Anger Means

At the Plaza Hotel in midtown Manhattan, Cary Grant requests coffee and a pair of English muffins for breakfast. When the order arrives, there's the coffee but only three half slices. The other half slice of a muffin is missing. Determined to get a satisfactory explanation, Grant asks the waiter, calls the head of room service, and so on, up the chain of command. Then the movie star insists on having a call put through to the hotel's owner, Conrad Hilton, in Beverly Hills, despite it being the crack of dawn in California. When Hilton proves to be in Istanbul, Turkey, Grant still won't relent and has Mr. Hilton called there, instead, to complain.

Where's my half slice? Hilton knows. A hotel efficiency expert has determined that most guests were leaving the fourth slice on their plates. So, why bother to serve it?

Welcome to anger, an emotion about wanting to be in control of your circumstances and make progress. In Grant's case, progress means the flurry of phone calls it takes to finally get an answer. Yes, the stakes are obviously small. But Grant's sense of having been taken advantage of, and determination to rectify matters, just as clearly looms large, no matter how zealously distorted his perspective might be.[1]

For this star of movies like *Bringing Up Baby* (1938) and *North by Northwest* (1959), what were the implications of wanting control? Start with being a well-known tightwad with money. Then add how Grant was so eager to dictate the behavior of the women in his life that his wife, Dyan Cannon, only half-jokingly called him "The Master."

As Cannon's rueful nickname for Grant implies, anger is often, at best, something of a mixed blessing. Anger is the most dominant, assertive emotion of the seven core emotions. It's also, like happiness and sadness, an approach emotion. In symbolic terms, rather than *to hug*, like happiness, or to be *longing for a hug*, like sadness, the essence of anger is *to hit*. Anger aids survival by enabling us to fight off threats or dismantle barriers that keep us from realizing our ambitions.

Although typically classified as a "negative" emotion, anger therefore joins the other so-called negative emotions in having an upside. Anger can help us eliminate a problem or pursue a superior solution. A person exhibiting this emotion is likely to be energetic and enterprising, focused and determined. Those qualities can be very attractive, at times.

Still, if someone's too hot-headed and grumpy, watch out. The reason most of us try to avoid physical fights is that we can never be sure if we will win and, even if we do win, whether we will come out of the fight seriously hurt. There can be more harm than gain, even as the supposed winner. Verbally expressed anger is cause for concern, too. Contrary to popular belief, anger is stoked instead of resolved by venting.[2] "Blowing off steam" can blow the whole place up, and with it the relationships we care about most.

Spotting Anger

Pick up early signs of this emotion in others and you may be able to defuse some situations before they get out of hand. That's the advantage of knowing an angry face *contracts* like a snake coiling to strike. People who get angry are aptly characterized as becoming red-faced and "boiling mad" because blood floods the face when they're incensed. More specifically, anger appears in nine ways on the face, including the following five ways when it's the only emotion being shown:

Eyes

The eyes narrow and the lower eyelids tighten and rise, narrowing the eyes.

Mouth

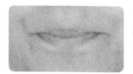 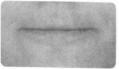 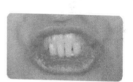

Mild anger: the lips narrow or compress and will also purse together.

Intense anger: the lips narrow even more and a bulge forms below the middle of the lower lip.

Extreme anger: very taut lips part and form a horizontal funnel, exposing the teeth.

Jaw & Chin

The entire jaw pushes forward and the chin sticks out.

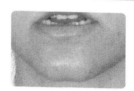

Next, there are four additional ways that anger gets expressed in tandem with other, specific emotions as listed below:

Eyebrows

The eyebrows come together and pull down, creating a vertical crease between the eyebrows.
(anger, fear, sadness)

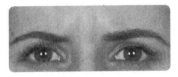

Eyes

The eyes go wide as the upper eyelids rise.
(anger, fear, surprise)

Cheeks & Mouth

The upper lip curls, the nostrils flare, and the skin pouches alongside the nose.
(anger, contempt, disgust)

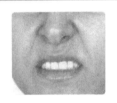

Mouth & Chin

The chin's dimpled skin rises and the mouth forms an upside-down smile.
(anger, disgust, sadness)

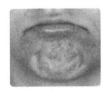

Most Angry

Eminem
Douglas MacArthur
Joseph McCarthy
John Bonham
Leonardo DiCaprio
Kanye West
George Wallace
Khloe Kardashian
Angelina Jolie
Robert Redford

Anger's Top 10 List

Anger appears in more ways on the face than any other core emotion, but it's not just versatile—it's also pervasive. Among the celebrities analyzed for *Famous Faces Decoded*, on average a little over 30% of their emoting involves anger. Of the seven emotions this book covers, only happiness is more common. As to the emotions that might be classified as "negative" feelings, the next most common is fear, with merely one-third the frequency of anger.

Do men get angry more often than women? Studies find that's true, in part because men place more importance on status and power. War, with its opportunities for changes in fortune, is anger taken to extremes.[3] In this book's 173-person sample, male celebrities show on average slightly more anger than their female counterparts and dominate the Top 10 list for Most Angry. Among them is somebody who's no stranger to war: General Douglas MacArthur.

In contrast, the Top 10 list for Least Angry is evenly split by gender and invites another way to look at anger. While excess anger can be detrimental, even fatal, a lack of anger can also have its shortcomings. Among other emotions that can also be motivating in their own way, anger helps you

Least Angry

Marilyn Monroe
Charles Schulz
Diane Keaton
Whitney Houston
Magic Johnson
Mary Lou Retton
Paul McCartney
Larry Page
John Lennon
Mariah Carey

protect and promote yourself, seizing opportunities when they emerge. Appearing on the Least Angry list is Diane Keaton, who in a 1978 *New Yorker* profile admits that by junior high school she was always auditioning, "but I didn't seem to have much drive. I still don't really have it."[4]

How good are people at spotting anger? Maybe because it can be life-threatening not to detect anger, people are pretty good at recognizing this emotion. At 55%, anger comes in third among eight emotional categories for its level of detection accuracy (behind both the mild and strong versions of happiness). Accordingly, for six of the ten celebrities who appear in the Top 10 Most Angry list, voters correctly picked up on the prevalence of their anger.

Eminem

Voted

anger
contempt

Actual

anger
fear

Rare

satisfaction

A case in point is Eminem. Here is how the rapper who became the best-selling musical artist of the 2000s in America has described his lyric-writing process: "If I'm mad at my girl, I'm gonna sit down and write the most misogynistic fucking rhyme in the world. It's not how I feel in general, it's how I feel at that moment."[5] Don't believe him. In actuality, Eminem is almost always angry; a staggering three-quarters of his emoting involves anger, often shown through a combination of tightened lower eyelids and lips firmly pressed together.

Khloe Kardashian

Voted

sadness
happiness

Actual

anger
acceptance

Rare

fear

By comparison, there were four other celebrities in the Top 10 Most Angry list that voters failed to assess well emotionally: Douglas MacArthur, Leonardo DiCaprio, Robert Redford, and finally Khloe Kardashian, who voters saw as mostly sad, not angry. I guess they missed the episode in season four of *Keeping Up with the Kardashians* where Khloe slaps somebody on-screen and gets sent to an anger management class.[6] That plot line faithfully reflects the tendency for Khloe's upper lip to curl in anger and her lower eyelids to grow tense when she's displeased, which is frequently.

What May Cause Anger

Check out Ranker's online list of people's favorite songs about anger. Aggression emerges as the de facto theme. In first place is "Killing in the Name" by Rage Against the Machine, and it goes on from there. Anger can occur for many reasons, as this set of seven likely causes makes clear.

1. We seek to control our circumstances, including resources.

Eminem's upbringing is bereft of financial resources or security. The future singer's drug-addled mom takes most of his teenage wages but still kicks him out of the house for not helping to support her. Eminem's dad is out of the picture so early Eminem never meets him. The artistic output that follows is "horror-core" humor, without limits, from a singer whose single most characteristic expression is a narrow, snake-eyes look. An example of Eminem's grim humor: on *The Slim Shady LP* (1999), his alter-ego dumps his murdered girlfriend in a lake, aided by their baby daughter. "We'll roll her off the dock," Eminem sings, adding, "No more fighting with Dad, no more restraining order." In an alternative world of *judges-be-damned*, it's as if Eminem's alter-ego Slim Shady is sanctioning murder as the ultimate form of control.

2. Kept from making progress toward a goal, we tend to become angrier the more we feel a barrier to progress is unfair.

In 1984 a nearly flawless John McEnroe is in the middle of a year in which his winning percentage will exceed 95%. The tennis star will conquer almost every event, including the Swedish Open. In Stockholm, however, McEnroe unleashes a monumental temper tantrum[7] triggered by a serve called "out". McEnroe's diatribe follows: "That ball was right on the line, *right* on the line. You've made no mistakes in this match yet, *right?*" This is McEnroe taunting the chair umpire, redirecting his competitive attention away from his opponent across the net (who remains the real barrier to victory in the match). Not waiting for an answer, McEnroe reiterates: "No mistakes *whatsoever*." When the umpire remains silent, McEnroe's eyes go wide, his lips part, his teeth get bared, and his lower lip turns out. Displaying the kind of a look you see when a dog is growling over a lost bone, the tennis star verbally unloads: *"Answer the question! The question, jerk!"*

Jeers and boos rain down from the Swedes filling the arena. The judge issues a code violation. In response, McEnroe smacks a ball into the bleachers at a loud-mouthed fan objecting to his outburst. Distracted or perhaps more like *unhinged*, McEnroe loses the next point and with it that game.

At the changeover, the violence gets worse. Gripping his tennis racket as if it's a golf club, McEnroe whacks his tennis bag. Then he hits a teeshot that connects with his water bottle, sending it into the air, across the front row of spectators. Water splatters the King of Sweden as it goes by. The judge screams *"Code violation!"* repeatedly as McEnroe starts swatting anything in reach. With a forehand swing, the left-hander destroys a courtside flower arrangement. Then finally spent from rage, McEnroe hides beneath a blue towel he drapes over his head in embarrassment as he sits down to regain some composure. Two years later, the burnt-out star takes a half-year sabbatical from tennis, signaling the end of his reign.

3. In reaction to feeling lost or confused, we focus on solving the problem.

After Angelina Jolie's parents divorce, a rocky relationship with her famous father, Jon Voight, doesn't help matters. The future actress's first career ambition as a teenager is to become a funeral director. From insomnia to depression so severe that Jolie tries to hire a hit man to end her life, upheaval consumes her. But starting with *Lara Croft: Tomb Raider* (2001), her breakthrough movie, Jolie finds professional success and settles into her tell-tale expression of anger: eyes narrowed in a piercing gaze that brings to mind a fire where you don't see the flames, but can smell the smoke beyond the next ridge of trees.

Not easy to typecast, Jolie has become a humanitarian advocate for conservation, education, women's rights, and refugees, all without entirely shedding her past. At the same time as promoting those warm-hearted causes, Jolie remains in her own words, "just a punk kid with tattoos," one of which declares: "What nourishes me destroys me." Go figure, or go search for clues in Jolie's past. Reverse the tattoo's motto by putting "destroys" ahead of "nourishes" and you've got another part of Jolie's teenage years. The actress admits to having once upon a time cut herself repeatedly because pain felt "somehow therapeutic to me."

4. To survive a challenge or threat, we go on the attack, possibly relieving stress.

For four long years in a row, Michael Jordan's challenge is to get his Chicago Bulls past the Detroit Pistons in the NBA's Eastern Conference play-offs. The "Bad Boys" Pistons enjoy roughing up Jordan and always win the head-to-head matchup, until at last in 1991 Jordan pushes himself and his teammates hard enough to prevail.

As dominant in practice as in actual games, Jordan punches two teammates in the face during scrimmages and taunts many others.[8] Among those under siege is "Medical Bill" Cartwright, as Jordan likes to call him. Believing Cartwright has "bad hands," Jordan throws him a series of impossible-to-catch passes that end when the center pulls Jordan aside and tells him to stop or else "you will never play basketball again because I will break both of your legs." A notoriously vindictive Hall of Fame speech in 2009, in which Jordan derides many former coaches, teammates, and even his own children, shows his Airness has not yet learned to ease up. It's a verdict supported by the many ways Jordan shows anger off-court, including: lowered eyebrows, tightened eyelids, and a flaring upper lip.

5. We resist the status quo or a change in circumstances, often because our expectations have been violated.

The put-down is that, over the years, critics' descriptions of Robert Redford suggest he's a somewhat bland, bankable "golden boy."[9] While no one particular form of anger most characterizes Redford, a look of lips firmly pressed together in annoyance come the closest. In response to being typecast, Redford wants more than merely to be seen as a safe-sex presence on-screen. He expects something more of himself. So even as Barbara Streisand, Redford's co-star in *The Way We Were* (1973), reportedly drools over filming scenes like their fireside courtship in Malibu, Redford is already aiming for something higher. For him the movie is really about "The questionable nature of true free speech," more so than being a steamy romance.

Not happy with Hollywood conventions, Redford has now long ago become an eco-activist and the creator of the alternative Sundance Film Festival in Utah. In doing so, he's supporting artistic endeavors that mirror his independent, *I-won't-buckle-under* mindset. Stubbornly resolved not to play the game the usual way, Redford has made all the money he might need and has moved on to striving for merit instead.

6. Feeling demeaned and resentful, we seek to preserve and enhance our own identity or that of a group to which we belong.

The son of a former Black Panther party member and an English literature professor, Kanye West advocates for what he calls examples of Black Excellence that will enhance his race's identity. West is also famously, even *notoriously* outspoken. That trait suits a guy whose signature expression of anger is the intense version in which firmly pressed lips cause a bulge to form below the lower lip. After Hurricane Katrina strikes New Orleans, West punctuates a live 2005 telethon for its victims by ad-libbing a comment that strikes many people as plausible given the sorry state of America's race relations, namely, "George Bush doesn't care about black people."

A second, surprising off-script moment occurs during the 2009 MTV Video Music Awards. The musician Taylor Swift has taken the stage to accept the award for Best Female Video for "You Belong with Me." Believing that Beyonce deserves the award for "Single Ladies (Put a Ring on It)," West responds by seizing the stage, grabbing the microphone from Swift, and proclaiming Beyonce's video "one of the best videos of all time." Again, the point is to challenge a status quo that favors whites. This injustice, however, doesn't match the scale of Katrina's aftermath. West's anger has gotten the better of him. In response, the musical artist gets banished for the remainder of that year's MTV show and called a "jackass" by President Barack Obama.

7. We fight against injustice, seeking to rectify situations that are contrary to our values.

It's fair to say that both men caught up in a nationally televised exchange during the Army-McCarthy Hearings of 1954 feel a sense of injustice. Prolonged, intense anger verging on rage belongs to only one man, though. That's Senator Joseph McCarthy, whose displays of anger overwhelmingly favor narrowed eyes. For McCarthy, the injustice is that he believes Communist traitors lurk inside the U.S. government. For his counterpart, the U.S. Army's chief legal counsel Joseph Welch, the injustice lies elsewhere. Welch believes McCarthy's hearings have become a witch hunt harming the lives of decent, patriotic Americans.

Their conflicting views come to a head when Welch says: "You've done enough. Have you no sense of decency, sir, at long last? Have you left no sense of decency?" Ducking the question, McCarthy patronizingly resumes by saying "I know this [line of questioning] hurts you, Mr. Welch."

Quick with a retort, Welch replies, "I'll say it hurts," which he offers with a sad, wistful smile and just a touch of anger.

Four Forms of Anger

A dog is a dog is a dog. Well, not really. As everyone knows, not all dogs in the park are as likely to growl at another dog as some are. Likewise, anger isn't a monolithic, one-size-fits-all emotion. While a testy Thunderstorm look might be vaguely comparable to a pit bull, the happiness-infused expression I'm calling the Golden Blend comes closer to being like a gentle Golden Retriever. The other two forms of anger fall somewhere in between that first pair in terms of their positive versus negative orientation.

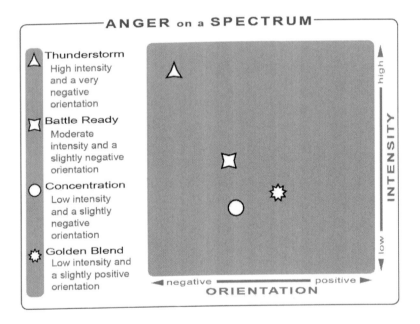

As the chart shows,[10] Thunderstorm is more intense as well as more negative than the other most assertive version of anger: Battle Ready. Both forms are nevertheless problematic. They most closely adhere to anger's *hit* instinct and are assertive, even hostile. Concentration and Golden

Blend are the remaining forms of anger, which involve more subdued, constructive reactions. Of them, Golden Blend qualifies as a slightly positive feeling because it mixes anger with mild happiness.

More specifically, each form of anger gets shown as follows:

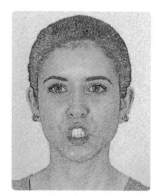

Thunderstorm

Thunderstorm: Sometimes, angry people's lips tighten so severely that a bulge forms below the center of their lower lip. Much less common is when their lips form a hyper-tense, teeth-bared growl, as is on display in this case. Either way, stay alert. Danger lurks. With the tell-tale bulge, also look for suddenly thin lips that may almost disappear from view. These visual clues serve as a warning that you may be physically or verbally struck.

Battle Ready: When people's upper eyelids rise, their eyes widen as if their eyeballs are protruding. At other times, the eyes may narrow while the lower eyelids grow tense. The most intimidating version of this look combines the two movements, as shown here with the upper eyelids raised and the lower eyelids tense. Then you're being stared down in a manner similar to how cats arch their backs to look larger and more intimidating in a hostile encounter.

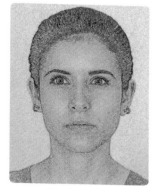

Battle Ready

Concentration: A less adversarial version of anger is when the eyebrows lower and knit together, creating a vertical wrinkle between them. The deeper the wrinkle and the more firmly someone's lips may simultaneously press together (short of forming the lower-lip bulge evident in the accompanying photo), the more that person is focused on the matter at hand. Note that a Concentration expression often reveals some confusion, as the puzzled person strives for clarity and a restored sense of control.

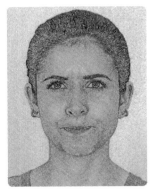

Concentration

Golden Blend

Golden Blend: A good strategy for coming across as powerful, yet not dangerous, is to blend anger and happiness. That emotional tandem combines backbone with warmth, evident in this example given the model's tight-lipped smile and narrowed eyes. Socially acceptable anger is anger that appears restrained and nicely balanced by happiness. Put yet another way, to combine a welcoming grin with signs of assertiveness demonstrates calm resolve.

Each Form's Top 10 List

How do anger's four forms apply to the celebrities facially coded for this book? The two more intense forms—Thunderstorm and Battle Ready—

are heavily represented by politicians in particular, but also by musicians. As for the two milder forms of anger (Concentration and Golden Blend), there Hollywood stars and, again, musicians are prevalent. With the Golden Blend form, media figures also become common, alongside a far greater number of female celebrities than is true of especially the more intense forms of anger. Angelina Jolie, Leonardo DiCaprio, Eminem, John Bonham, and Douglas MacArthur all appear twice across these four Top 10 lists.

Thunderstorm: Among the celebrities prone to this expression is Hillary Clinton. It's entirely possible to imagine such a look of grim determination on her face during a famous scene in Joe Klein's *Primary Colors*,[11] a thinly disguised novel about Bill and Hillary Clinton. I'm referring to the moment when the character almost certainly modeled on Hillary says to her husband: "You could have been such a great president if you weren't such an undisciplined shit." Note that both members of this power couple appear in the Top 10 list for Thunderstorm.

TOP 10

Thunderstorm

Jimmy Page
Kanye West
Joe Frazier
Bill Clinton
Donald Trump
Rush Limbaugh
Peyton Manning
Jeb Bush
Hillary Clinton
Barack Obama

Who are the other celebrities filling out the list? Those most prone to this lashing, forceful version of anger range from heavy-metal, Led Zeppelin guitarist Jimmy Page; to a former heavy-weight boxing champion, Smokin' Joe Frazier; and enough politicians to remind us that politics is often called a blood sport. Fully half the list is taken up by politicians, among them three candidates from 2016: Donald Trump, Hillary Clinton, and an often straining, deeply frustrated Jeb Bush.

Battle Ready

Eminem
Joseph McCarthy
James Dean
Angelina Jolie
Charles Manson
Michael Milken
Kurt Cobain
Taylor Swift
Roger Clemens
Jack Welch

Battle Ready: High on the Top 10 list of those Battle Ready is Joseph McCarthy. Anger constitutes over 60% of his entire emoting, double the average for the celebrities in *Famous Faces Decoded*. "McCarthyism is Americanism with its sleeves rolled up" is how the Senator once described his style of going after alleged Communists during the 1950s Red Scare that he avidly promoted. Implicit in "sleeves rolled up" was McCarthy's eagerness for a fight. The hearings he held were almost like televised boxing matches, with witnesses either fighting off or succumbing to McCarthy's verbal punches.

This Top 10 list is full of compelling figures. For example, besides two convicts—mass murderer Charles Manson, and former junk bond king Michael Milken—there's General Electric's former CEO, Jack Welch. How did Welch earn the intimidating nickname "Neutron Jack"? In downsizing the company's ranks, Welch would fire any employee caught in the bottom 10% of GE's annual performance reviews.

Concentration: One example of a celebrity favoring the Concentration look is Tom Hanks, who has admitted that "Everybody has something that chews them up and, for me, that

Concentration

Douglas MacArthur
Jay-Z
John Bonham
Eminem
George H. W. Bush
Ronald Reagan
George Harrison
Johnny Cash
Leonardo DiCaprio
Tom Hanks

thing was always loneliness." Many a time, though, he reinforces isolation by not saying much, especially to the media. Seen by voters surveyed for *Famous Faces Decoded* as happy and happier, a nice, trustworthy guy, Hanks's version of anger involves maintaining control and self-control alike. For instance, Hanks tells a *Guardian* journalist[12] he's happy to talk "about absolutely anything." Queries lead to answers that stymie the journalist, and Hanks even pretends not to hear some questions—so resistant is he to sharing anything that would make good copy.

The epitome of someone being either well focused or at times too narrowly focused, the Concentration form features a Top 10 list that consists entirely of male celebrities. Well focused? That might be Leonardo DiCaprio, who has admitted to being "unhappy doing things that I'm not passionate about." As a candidate for too narrowly focused, consider Douglas MacArthur. The general's insistence on pushing his U.S. troops ever farther north during the Korean War brought China into the conflict.

Golden Blend: Even though she didn't quite qualify for this Top 10 list, Taylor Swift has adeptly embodied the Golden Blend look on her way to becoming a one-woman musical empire. Her statement that "Careers take hard work" fits her frequent combination of a pert smile and a steely, eyes-narrowed gaze. An album and a concert tour titled *Fearless* (2008) surely overstate Swift's degree of equanimity. Nevertheless, she's intrepid in carving out a path for herself. More angry than happy, Swift mostly shows slight smiles in keeping with her recent remark: "In terms of being happy, I've never been closer to that."[13]

TOP 10

Golden Blend

Estee Lauder
Khloe Kardashian
Douglas MacArthur
Angelina Jolie
Amy Schumer
Kim Kardashian
Leonardo DiCaprio
John Bonham
J. K. Rowling
Edward Snowden

The Top 10 list for Golden Blend is loaded with female talent. Besides Amy Schumer and her zinging humor, add Estee Lauder and, two generations later, the likewise enterprising Kardashian sisters: Khloe and Kim. Finally, there's J. K. Rowling, the very rare case of an author rewarded for her talent by becoming a billionaire.

Summary

Anger and ambition often fit like a glove. When we want to get things done, remove barriers to progress, and exert control over our destiny, anger can come in handy. Then it might serve as the rocket fuel that keeps us focused. Anger epitomizes getting our hands—and fists—around a problem to solve our dilemma. So far so good, perhaps, but implicit in my reference to *fists* is why anger can also be so problematic. This emotion is functionally suited to help us hit out at people, objects, and viewpoints we consider to be blocking our progress and preferences.

By helping us fight off threats, and thereby survive and thrive, anger is central to life and a frequent emotion that the male celebrities in this book show a little more often than their female counterparts. In anger, the face's muscles contract and tense up. We're preparing for conflict and not open to others, who commonly get viewed as opponents to conquer. With anger, people skills suffer. So while this emotion can energize us in fighting against injustices, the presence of anger also means that securing a desired outcome can take precedence over showing concern for the individuals involved.

Happiness

The Luxury Emotion

What Happiness Means

It's known as *Ellen's* "Puppy Episode." Ratings are down and desperate to achieve its version of happiness (commercial success), the network proposes introducing a puppy as a love interest for the show's star. In contrast, Ellen DeGeneres is seeking personal happiness and prefers an authentic love interest. Ready to "out" herself, she pushes for a script full of halting and apprehensive dialogue, leading to self-confession.[1] Here, DeGeneres's character Ellen Morgan is talking to Susan, who has only recently revealed she's a lesbian and admitted she thought Ellen was one, too.

Ellen: You know how you said in the room, you know, that you thought, maybe I was ... I was thinking about it, and ...

Susan: Are you saying what I think you're trying to say?

Ellen: What do you think I'm trying to say?

Susan: Oh, I'm not going to say it again and be wrong.

Ellen: No, you're not wrong. You're right. This is so hard … I'm
           so afraid to tell people. I mean … I'm just … Susan …

Then just as Ellen is turning back toward Susan, she puts one hand on a service counter and accidentally presses the airport's PA system, making a private moment *very* public.

Ellen: I'm gay.

With that admission, a huge, beaming smile flashes across Ellen's face. Welcome to happiness! This emotion is basically a "me"-"we" proposition. People feel their happiest when they're being true to their own values (me) and are simultaneously supported, externally, by others (we) who endorse them for being who they genuinely are. In this case, DeGeneres has affirmed her sexual orientation. By doing so, she's cleared the path to realizing a greater degree of fulfillment, which is what happiness is about. In affirming oneself and, in effect, hugging oneself, a person can become more emotionally available to others, too.

Because the essence of happiness is to *hug* oneself as well as other people, it could almost go without saying that happiness is an approach emotion. Happiness brings people together. It's a matter of affection and affiliation. Happiness helps individuals approach situations, social or otherwise, as opportunities to be embraced, rather than as risks to be avoided.

Like anger, happiness qualifies as a dominant, approach emotion. The difference between the two feelings is vast, however, in regards to tonality and intent. While anger is aggressively dominant, imposing itself on others, happiness is *affirmatively* dominant. With happiness, people are invited to bask in its warm glow. The only facial display capable of being seen at distances of as great as 300 feet,[2] robust smiles foster cooperation, serving as the emotional equivalent of a "Welcome, Open for Business" sign.

Put so simply, happiness may seem like an easily realized emotion. But as Woody Allen has joked, "Happiness makes up in height what it lacks in length." Of the seven core emotions, happiness emerges as the one clearly upbeat emotional sensation. Why does it stand alone? The answer is that from a survival point of view, *life is hard and then you die*. In other words, happiness could be considered a luxury emotion—not as vital as the other, "negative" emotions that assist us in handling challenges.

Nevertheless, happiness isn't a trivial emotion. Thomas Jefferson enshrined "Life, Liberty and the pursuit of Happiness" in America's Declaration of Independence, and none of us wants to go without happiness if we have anything to say in the matter.

Happy people aren't just happy. Studies indicate that happy people tend to live longer and be more creative—brainstorming superior solutions more quickly than those who are less content.[3] Like all emotions, happiness is contagious. So an opportunity to be around cheerful, optimistic people can feel good, making happy people a magnet for attention. Who doesn't want the glow of happiness? And who doesn't harbor the hope of future happiness, however fleeting?

Spotting Happiness

A happy face *lifts up* as if a flower welcoming the sun. More specifically, happiness appears in only two ways on the face: look for when twinkling eyes narrow and the skin below them bags or wrinkles; as well as when the corners of the mouth turn up, causing the cheeks to lift.

To detect those few signals sounds easy enough, now doesn't it? In order for you to fully grasp how happiness works, though, I want to share a secret I've learned from my two decades of facial coding: happiness is actually *four slightly different but equally essential feelings rolled up into one emotion*. To tease out the various manifestations of happiness, let's delve deeper into this emotion's *four levels*: joy and pleasure (again as noted in the introduction, both qualify as strong *happiness* with asterisks if appearing in a celebrity's emotional profile); and satisfaction and acceptance (both qualify as merely mild happiness, appearing without asterisks, in any of the voted, actual, or rare results).

How does each level of happiness get revealed?

Eyes, Cheeks & Mouth

The highest level of happiness is joy, which can't be faked. When you're exuberantly happy, the muscle around the eyes constricts, causing not only twinkling eyes but also the skin around the eyes to bag, wrinkle, and change their shape. Another change is that crow's feet often emerge at the outer corner of the eyes. All of this activity is accompanied by a smile and usually a pronounced lifting of the cheeks.

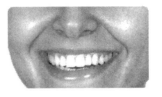

Cheeks & Mouth

The second highest level of happiness is pleasure. In this case, there's no gleam in the eye but there's still a big (often toothy) grin that lifts the cheeks until they touch or almost touch the eye sockets.

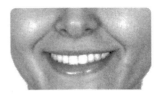

Cheeks & Mouth

The third level of happiness is satisfaction. These are either subdued, genuine smiles or social smiles: instances where people may not feel very happy but manage a smile when told to say "Cheese". With these smiles, the cheeks will only rise slightly. The satisfaction version of happiness requires looking for how the corners of the mouth lift just enough to clearly signal a smile.

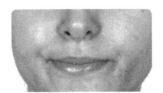

Mouth

The lowest level of happiness is acceptance. While the cheeks barely move, if at all, one or both corners of the mouth rise ever so slightly. An acceptance-level smile still signals happiness, but of the grimmest sort. A Thomas Hardy poem describes this look: "The smile on your mouth was the deadest thing / Alive enough to have strength to die."[4]

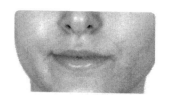

Happiness's Top 10 List

While only contempt shows up in as few places on the face as happiness, it's no contest between those two feelings when it comes to frequency. Among the celebrities facially coded for *Famous Faces Decoded*, almost 35% of their emoting involves happiness. It's the single most common emotion among the seven core emotions, edging out anger, which comes in second for frequency. Together, happiness and anger constitute two-thirds of all the emotions coded for this book.

Within my 173-person sample, which gender shows more happiness? The answer is women by a wide margin, with joy and acceptance being the levels at which the female celebrities notably outdistance their male counterparts. No single explanation covers the reasons why. To this day, though, it's probably fair to suggest that women may get routinely judged more favorably based

TOP 10
Most Happy

Ellen DeGeneres
Charles Schulz
John Lennon
Mariah Carey
Mary Lou Retton
Martha Stewart
Diane Keaton
Magic Johnson
David Letterman
Jim Henson

TOP 10

Least Happy

Donald Trump
Aaron Rodgers
Barack Obama
Eminem
George H. W. Bush
Cam Newton
Johnny Cash
Douglas MacArthur
Hillary Clinton
Charles Manson

in part on their emotional warmth, whereas for men it's more likely to be their degree of self-assertion. Put another way, at least trying to appear happy is probably more important for the typical woman.

The greater prevalence for happiness among women is revealed in the Top 10 list for Most Happy. Female celebrities represent about a third of the celebrities facially coded for my sample, but they hold down half of these top ten slots. In contrast, the list of the Least Happy celebrities contains only one woman, Hillary Clinton, who comes in 9th in a list headlined by her 2016 election foe: Donald Trump.

Overall, in *Famous Faces Decoded* the emotions of anger and happiness, *to hit* or *to hug*, split by gender. In terms of which feeling the celebrities display most often, the men favor anger and the women various levels of happiness.

Since robust smiles are the only facial display readily evident at a distance, it shouldn't come as a shock that people are good at recognizing happiness. At 84% accuracy, mild happiness comes in first in terms of strength of detection, with strong *happiness* second best given a 68% accuracy rate.

It therefore follows that every celebrity in the Top 10 Most Happy list was correctly deemed

Mary Lou Retton

Voted

happiness surprise

Actual

joy *pleasure*

Rare

anger

by voters as being distinguished by their happiness, with only the degree of happiness being at issue. For example, voters indeed saw in Mary Lou Retton the natural exuberance that made the gymnast a crowd favorite during the 1984 Summer Olympics. No wonder she became the first female athlete ever to grace the front of a Wheaties box. With her gleaming, often eye-twinkling smile, Retton couldn't help but attract fans. In a 1993 sports study, she was still tied for first as America's most popular athlete.

Mariah Carey

Voted

happiness
sadness

Actual

pleasure
joy

Rare

anger

As for Mariah Carey, the earpiece malfunction that doomed her New Year's Eve 2017 concert in Times Square, causing Carey to walk off the stage in a huff, isn't as representative of her emoting as are the smiles of joyfulness and pleasure she displays. Voters saw mild happiness, along with sadness, as being characteristic of Carey. The reality is greater bliss, however, as befits the woman whose 1995 hit single "One Sweet Day" remains America's longest-running, number-one song ever.

What May Cause Happiness

Let's briefly revisit *Ellen's* "Puppy Episode." Imagine you're the show's director and lately your star hasn't been the same. Not only are the ratings down, but Ellen DeGeneres is unhappy that the U.S. Congress passed the Defense of Marriage Act a year ago. Her suggestion to "out" herself inspires the biggest true smile you've seen from DeGeneres in quite some time. Are you going to turn down her idea or take it to the network's executives?

In weighing your choice, you're wise to the various reasons why happiness emerges.

1. We're suddenly more fulfilled, having experienced some kind of success or improvement in our circumstances. (Pride is a likely, related feeling in this case.)

No, no, I'm really him, Charles Schulz finds himself insisting at his Central High School class reunion in St. Paul, Minnesota. Nobody believes him. So finally Schulz proves he really is the *Peanuts* cartoonist by drawing Charlie Brown for the former classmates gathered around him. It isn't the first time Schulz has been doubted. When he proposed to the woman on whom his comic strip character Lucy is likely modeled, her mom intervened. Told that Schulz wouldn't amount to much, the woman married a fireman instead.[5] Twenty years later, *Happiness Is a Warm Puppy* (1962) has hit the best-seller list. The previously hardscrabble, often gloomy Schulz is now a rich, radiantly smiling man. He's got both a twinkle in his eyes and a bank account that's growing by over $30 million a year.

2. We harbor reasonable hope for the future, having made progress toward a goal we have. Optimism seems warranted. (Relief is a likely, related feeling in this case.)

At a Christie's auction of Hollywood memorabilia in 1999, Mariah Carey picks up for $662,500 a chipped, white baby grand piano that had belonged to Marilyn Monroe's mother "and was a piece of" the actress's childhood. Why the purchase? For starters, Monroe is the namesake of Carey's daughter and Carey's biggest inspiration. So while Carey won't ever play the purchased piano, or even tune it, she's bought it to preserve "what she [Marilyn] cared about."[6]

More deeply, however, the piano calls to mind for Carey her own childhood instability. Her parents' divorce when Carey was three years old led to a childhood in which Carey, her mom, and siblings moved together through a string of 13 marginal homes across Long Island. Nowadays, Monroe's piano serves as a touchstone for Carey, a way to stay grounded. The singer is happy and grateful for her success, often flashing large smiles, while mindful of how sad life can sometimes be.

3. We've achieved security and are no longer surrendering to circumstances beyond our control. Certainty brings comfort.

Convicted of insider stock trading in 2004 and sentenced to a five-month term in a federal correctional facility, Martha Stewart faces for the first time ever doubters about the on-going viability of her one-woman business empire. How wrong those doubters prove to be. Soon, Stewart is active again in her magazine, *Martha Stewart Living*, which might as well be renamed *Martha Stewart Working* given her copious output. Besides a wealth of other products, Stewart even begins to sell a line of homes modeled on her private estates. To focus on the merchandise alone misses the underlying point, however. As Stewart notes, her version of domestic order means gladly offering "not a fantasy, but a reality that looks like a fantasy." In supporting her brand, Stewart reveals in photographs a penchant for big pleasure smiles, the second highest level of happiness. In contrast, eye-twinkling joy eludes Stewart as much as her taking a rest from her many endeavors.

4. Our identity gets affirmed, individually or as part of a group. We experience a sense of belonging, whether based on family, friends, or romantic bonds. We've begun to feel cared about.

While Brian Epstein at first manages The Beatles, and George Martin becomes their producer, the band's leader is unquestionably John Lennon. Lennon formed the band's various lineups beginning in 1957 and urged The Beatles on with the promise they were headed "for the top." Now they're stars, and as my chart Beatles' Emotions Through the Years shows, Lennon is enjoying their early success the most. Granted, he rarely hits the high note of true, joyful smiles. But for a guy whose seaman father wandered off and mom died early, hit by a car, Lennon must find solace in being, as Paul McCartney later acknowledges, the one "we all looked up to" within a tight, cohesive group.[7]

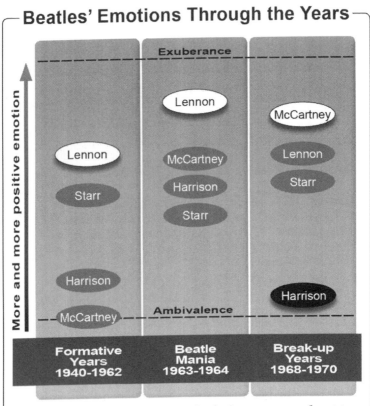

Beatles' Emotions Through the Years

More and more positive emotion

Exuberance

Lennon	Lennon	McCartney
Starr	McCartney	Lennon
	Harrison	Starr
	Starr	
Harrison		
McCartney	Ambivalence	Harrison

Formative Years 1940-1962	Beatle Mania 1963-1964	Break-up Years 1968-1970

Who among The Beatles shows the highest amount of positive emoting, and during which era of the band? John Lennon was the group's leader and its happiest member until things went awry, with Paul McCartney then taking the happiness lead instead.

Later, the dynamic changes. First, George Harrison in 1968, followed by Lennon in 1969, each momentarily leaves the band before being coaxed back. When The Beatles officially break up in 1970, McCartney will explain (and complain): "I didn't leave The Beatles. The Beatles have left."

In the band's final stage, McCartney emerges as the happiest Beatle, usurping Lennon's role as the group's cheerleader. Cajoling the others to rediscover their group spirit has become the veiled message in McCartney songs like "Get Back." Trying to direct Lennon, however, is doomed to fail. In the end, Lennon objects to McCartney's departure notice, saying: "I started the band. I disbanded it. It's as simple as that." Well, actually it isn't quite that simple. During the break-up years, Harrison leaves The Beatles first in terms of feeling much less positive than his bandmates.

5. We indulge in sensory delight, and in whatever is amusing or introduces variety. We relish both the moment and any pleasing distractions.

When Julia Child is cooking in Paris, her husband Paul notices that his six feet, two inches tall wife is often stirring a pot she stoops to reach. So when they move to America, Paul designs a more suitable kitchen that becomes the setting for Child's in-home TV shows, starting with *The French Chef* in 1963.

It isn't just the food she cooks that Child finds delicious.[8] In describing her house in Cambridge, Massachusetts, on camera, Child says in her breathy, warbly voice: "If we could just have the kitchen and the bedroom, that would be all we'd need." Another time, she writes her husband: "I want to see you, touch you, kiss you, talk with you, eat with you, … eat you, maybe." To a city near where the Puritans had landed, Child brings a joyful, eye-twinkling determination not to "cater to the flimsies," those who only go halfway, in whatever room of the house.

6. Finding a purpose larger than ourselves gives life meaning.

It's 1963 and Gloria Steinem, who by her nature favors modest, satisfaction-level smiles, isn't currently very happy. Then again, Steinem's not experiencing her undercover, freelance journalism assignment as a Playboy Bunny for the fun of it. The future cofounder of *Ms.* magazine has something more in mind. In publishing a two-part exposé in *Show* magazine, she's offering a reality check on Hugh Hefner's monthly essays dubbed "the Emancipation Proclamation of the sexual revolution." Steinem's happiness comes, in this case, from knowing the gig's grin-and-bear-it hassles are ultimately worthwhile.

What is involved?[9] After getting tested for venereal diseases, Steinem receives her Bunny outfit. The shoes with their three-inch heels are so agonizing that after two weeks on the job, Steinem's feet will forever remain half a size larger. Meanwhile, the corset is easily at least two inches too small, except the bust, which gets issued with only D-cups. All in all, the outfit is so tight that even to sneeze might break the corset's zipper. As for filling the D-cups, like almost all of her new colleagues, Steinem resorts to stuffing them. The options are many: sanitary napkins, gym socks, and the solution the New York City Playboy Club's wardrobe mistress imposes on Steinem. A pair of plastic, dry-cleaning bags help to fill her costume.

"Sir, you are not allowed to touch the Bunnies" is the refrain taught in the orientation lecture for the latest hires. In reality, however, saying "no" doesn't do any good because the men continually try anyway and, when rebuffed, they will tweak Steinem's tail as she walks by. Once, when she rejects a customer's advance, he angrily responds: "What do you think I come here for, the roast beef?" On Steinem's final evening of duty, she overhears a fellow Bunny say of a customer, "He's a real gentleman. He treats you just the same whether you've slept with him or not." Thereby confirmed is Steinem's conclusion that a male-defined sexual revolution leaves plenty to be desired.

The aftermath of the exposé's publication is that, at first, Steinem is miserable. Hefner will claim that Playboy Bunny recruiting perversely improves, despite the bad publicity; and Steinem gets endless requests to repeat the feat, only this time as a prostitute. Offered an advance for a book that would transform her recent undercover experience into a lush romantic fantasy, Steinem returns the money. On the other hand, Steinem can ultimately say she's glad she wrote her famous scoop because "My exposé of working in a Playboy Club has outlived all the Playboy Clubs, both here and abroad."

7. We believe opportunity exists as part of a society where people largely play by the rules and there's a sufficient degree of justice.

That opportunity exists, Beyonce has never had cause to doubt. "I grew up upper-class. Private school. My dad had a Jaguar. We're African-American, and we work together as a family,"[10] Beyonce has said of her upbringing. Her childhood home was something of a showpiece. Picture a four-bedroom, brick-and-stucco mansion made possible by both her father's work as a salesman, first for Xerox and later for Johnson & Johnson, and her mother owning a highly successful hair salon. A work ethic that leads to success has been the hallmark of Beyonce's life. "Repetition, repetition," her father, Matthew, would preach after he left his job to manage Beyonce's first (childhood) band, Destiny's Child. To this day Beyonce repeatedly works and reworks her act. I'm never satisfied," she says, adding: "I've never met anyone that works harder than me in my industry."

At the same time, though, does Beyonce believe that opportunity broadly exists within a society where if people play by the rules, they can count on justice? Not exactly. Increasingly, Beyonce may flash joyful smiles while singing her songs but she hovers more in the range of acceptance-level smiles when she raises issues on stage like, "Do you want your daughter to have 75 cents when she deserves $1?" Politeness and success aren't a natural pairing, a sad truth Beyonce credits her dad for helping her first realize regarding the cutthroat world of entertainment.

Four Forms of Happiness

Go down the cereal aisle in your local grocery store, and every box with a cartoon character—from Tony the Tiger to Capt'n Crunch—will be the happiest person ever to appear at a breakfast table. To interject some realism, let's be honest: many people aren't exactly thrilled to pull themselves out of bed in the morning. If they do smile at dawn, those smiles won't be ear-to-ear grins but, rather, instances of mild happiness.

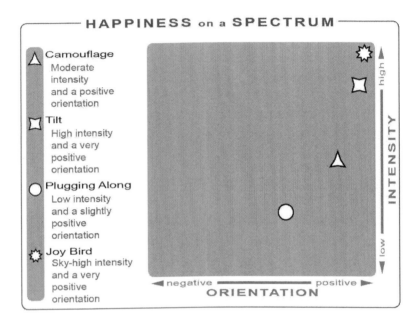

HAPPINESS on a SPECTRUM

Camouflage
Moderate intensity and a positive orientation

Tilt
High intensity and a very positive orientation

Plugging Along
Low intensity and a slightly positive orientation

Joy Bird
Sky-high intensity and a very positive orientation

INTENSITY — high / low

ORIENTATION — ◄ negative ========= positive ►

Earlier, I introduced four levels of happiness: joy, pleasure, satisfaction, and acceptance. Now I'm taking those four levels of happiness and putting one level of smiling front and center per form. In simplest terms, Camouflage equates to satisfaction smiles; Plugging Along to acceptance smiles; and Joy Bird to—what else—joyful smiles. More specifically, the more a celebrity favors a certain level of happiness *over time*—versus a *low* volume of the other three levels of happiness—the more that celebrity exemplifies a particular form of happiness. The exception is Tilt, which occurs when joy and pleasure (both strong levels of happiness) aren't *equally* shown over time.

In order, the first two forms of happiness in my chart, Camouflage and Tilt, reveal that this emotion can be less straightforward than you might have expected. Be alert whenever you encounter people emoting in these ways; what you see may *not* be what you get. Happiness isn't always pure sunshine. In contrast, the last two forms of happiness, Plugging Along and Joy Bird, are straightforward ones you can rely on.

More specifically, each form of happiness gets shown as follows:

Camouflage

Camouflage: These instances involve people who show lots of satisfaction, while also being at low volume for all of the other levels of happiness. Satisfaction smiles can be due to polite reserve. But if people are trying to ingratiate themselves with others or hide their true (negative) feelings with a smile, satisfaction-level smiles serve as social smiles. Then they become a matter of camouflage: a technique commonly used by people and animals alike to protect themselves from "predators". (The obvious comparison here is celebrities trying to ward off the paparazzi.) In this case, the accompanying photo has a modest smile tempered by a little anger.

With Camouflage comes complexity. Yes, happiness might seem like the easiest gig in town among the seven core emotions. How can you get a smile wrong? Think again; with smiles frequently deployed to bond with others and *deflect* trouble, watch out. Social smiles definitely pose the risk of not being detected for what they may actually be: less a matter of happiness than of masking adverse reactions.

Tilt: Okay, hang in there with me on my next explanation. To understand if people exhibit Tilt, you need an emotional baseline. What's their happiness emoting pattern over time? Do they exhibit lots of joy, but not much pleasure. Or is it the reverse? They show lots of pleasure, but not much

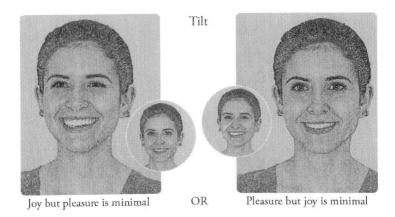

Tilt

Joy but pleasure is minimal   OR   Pleasure but joy is minimal

joy? (Both options are illustrated here.) When you recognize a disparity involving strong happiness, you've found a case of Tilt. Something is out of balance whenever the two highest levels of happiness being expressed by people, over time, vary a lot in terms of frequency. That one level is largely, curiously absent hints at instability. Be alert for an unresolved tension in people exhibiting this form of happiness, a tension that begs the question: why the huge imbalance?

Plugging Along: What if people show plenty of acceptance-level smiles, while the other three levels of happiness rarely occur? An acceptance smile is a mere toehold of receptivity, akin to *that's the worst joke I ever heard but at least you tried to humor me.* Habitually expressed, such a smile might also bring to mind Garrison Keillor's radio show quip about a reserved Norwegian-American man who "loved his wife so much he almost told her." While acceptance smiles represent the lowest, most begrudging level of happiness, there is nevertheless an upside to them. People who barely smile often plug

Plugging Along

along in a quiet, steady manner. They don't go too high or too low emotionally, and are unlikely to oversell themselves. Such a smile may be slight but carries across the mouth, as in this photo; or it may be unilateral and occupy just one corner of the mouth.

Joy Bird: To qualify, people will be unusually given to broad, joyful smiles, complete with twinkling eyes (like shown here), and do so in greater proportion than they show other levels of happiness. They're signaling rapture. It's hard to dislike Joy Birds, unless you're indulging in envy. These proverbial happy campers tend to be elastic in their thinking and

Joy Bird

may also exhibit a great ability to schmooze. Yet even this strongest form of happiness has a potential downside: happiness can leave us unfocused.

That caveat aside, what is it about joy that makes it special? Joy is a social magnet. The old cliché, "Smile, and the world smiles with you; cry, and you cry alone," didn't come about by chance.

Joyful smiles help people make their way through uncomfortable situations. Such smiles say *winner,* echoing why a female peacock chooses the male with the most dazzling plumage. Beautiful feathers showcase a male who will be a strong, healthy partner. With people, in turn, joyful smiles can offer the prospect of sharing in the victor's good fortune.

Each Form's Top 10 List

How do happiness's four forms apply to the celebrities facially coded for this book? The two forms that involve more complex, less straightforward displays of happiness—Camouflage and Tilt—are heavily represented by musicians (like John Lennon), and to a lesser extent by athletes and business people. With the other two forms of Plugging Along and Joy Bird, musicians and athletes remain common. In addition to Lennon, other celebrities making a pair of appearances across these four Top 10 lists are Bill Wyman, Mark Zuckerberg, Jack Welch, and Ellen Degeneres. Nearly half of the female celebrities represented across these four lists are famous for their roles on television.

Camouflage: Camouflage smiles suggest being able to navigate socially in a calculating manner. No surprise, Kim Kardashian has proven to be the most adroit of the Kardashian sisters—boosting her status through not only the TV series *Keeping Up with the Kardashians*, but also a home-sex video, and a book of selfies entitled *Selfish*.[11] Now Kim Kardashian-West after her marriage to Kanye West, she's the star whose fans sometimes include girls wearing t-shirts that say, "All Hail KKW."[12] Of evenings that were once

TOP 10
Camouflage
John Lennon
Larry Ellison
Jeb Bush
Peyton Manning
Chuck Berry
Ray Croc
Lindsey Vonn
Kim Kardashian
Ringo Starr
Cam Newton

spent partying with current frenemy Paris Hilton, Kardashian-West recalls: "We knew exactly where to go, where to be seen, how to have something written about you."

Who are the other celebrities joining the Top 10 list for Camouflage? Bandmates John Lennon and Ringo Starr appear, an outcome that might in part reflect their learning to mug for the cameras during the media blitz they faced as The Beatles. Also here is somebody who knows TV camera crews as well as Kardashian-West does: former NFL star quarterback Peyton Manning, now one of America's preeminent pitchmen.

Tilt

Ellen DeGeneres
Mark Zuckerberg
David Letterman
Bill Wyman
Whitney Houston
Jack Welch
Bill Cosby
John Lennon
Jennifer Aniston
Joe Montana

Tilt: A notable example of Tilt is Whitney Houston, whose immense talent was greater than her emotional stability. Pleasure, yes, but rarely did joy characterize her feelings in even her happiest moments. Gifted with an incredible voice, beauty, a mother who sang behind Aretha Franklin and Elvis Presley, Dionne Warwick for a cousin, and Darlene Love as her godmother, Houston had it all. But against her parents' wishes, she married a "street guy" named Bobby Brown. Then Whitney's childhood nickname, Nippy, alluding to a comic strip character prone to problems, quickly became prophetic.

Among the biggest Tilt celebrities are two linked to substance abuse: Houston, with her serious drug habit; and David Letterman, a recovering alcoholic. Also here is Bill Cosby, embroiled in sexual misconduct allegations. Then there is John Lennon, whose first solo album after The Beatles broke up featured therapeutic primal screaming as a way to cope with his mother's early death.

Plugging Along: Atop the list for Plugging Along is Amy Schumer. Opposed to idle chitchat due to an "insatiable" work ethic,[13] she instead favors what caused her breakthrough on *Last Comic Standing*: "I kept it

Plugging Along

Amy Schumer
Angelina Jolie
Bernie Madoff
Douglas MacArthur
John Bonham
Steven Spielberg
Andy Warhol
Dustin Hoffman
Elton John
Jimmy Page

honest on the show and it served me well." In that vein, these are Schumer's takes on a variety of topics. On Hollywood schmoozing: "I don't pretend to be nice." On childhood: "It was a 24-hour comedy boot camp in our house ... but for really sad reasons." And on hooking up: "I always thought sex was funny." After being photographed nude by Annie Liebowitz, Schumer tweeted her photo, writing: "Beautiful, gross, strong, thin, fat, pretty, ugly, sexy, disgusting, flawless, woman. Thank you." Can you see why you might expect slight, wry smiles from this comedian?

Likewise on the Top 10 list for Plugging Along is Steven Spielberg. As is true of Schumer, with Spielberg exuberance is eclipsed by getting the work done. In hindsight, Spielberg dismisses most of his creative efforts as "sugar substitutes."[14] Typically what you get with this director is a whisper of a smile and low, long tracking shots that simulate a world in which challenges loom large, but not insurmountable.

Joy Bird: Sure, being one of the richest people on earth doesn't hurt. But I believe joy would still define Mark Zuckerberg's manner, for better or worse, even without the money. Joy gives Zuckerberg the flair, the energy to climb the next mountain. Joy can at times, however, also cause him to be surprisingly blasé about key details. For instance, in *Chaos Monkeys*[15] a former Facebook staffer describes how hard it was to get Zuckerberg to focus on something that was hardly a minor matter: monetizing the company's user base prior to its IPO. Although *follow the money* is the lifeline of business, apparently Zuckerberg isn't always willing or able to adhere to that dictum.

TOP 10

Joy Bird

Ellen DeGeneres
Mark Zuckerberg
Jack Welch
Little Richard
Barack Obama
Mary Lou Retton
Bill Wyman
Michael Phelps
LeBron James
Tiger Woods

Others on this Top 10 list radiate "sweet dreams." They've achieved greater success than they could have ever imagined, and now they can bask and relax in its glow. That's especially true of Ellen DeGeneres, whose way forward in life wasn't obvious back when she held a variety of jobs ranging from being a waitress at T.G.I. Friday's to a vacuum cleaner saleswoman. It's likewise true of much-beloved Mary Lou Retton, whose big break came when an opening was created for her on the U.S. gymnastics squad because a teammate got injured prior to the 1984 Summer Olympics.

Summary

The rule of thumb is that once our basic needs are met, then the pursuit of happiness can rightly assume ever greater importance in our lives. But studies show that happiness benefits our physical, psychological, and social well-being at *all* times. Smiles make things happen—helping us, in part, through making a positive impression on others. Everyone likes to feel welcomed, and smiles do a nice job of it. Providing an emotional high that's often contagious, happiness enables us to bond with others.

In mind/body terms, smiling literally cools the head and creates a sense of comfort. People who are happy won't struggle to maintain their vigor due to lost hope. They will instead believe effort matters. The single most frequent of the seven core emotions celebrities show in *Famous Faces Decoded,* happiness gets displayed by the women here far more than by their male, play-it-cool counterparts.

Sadness

A Rear View Mirror

What Sadness Means

His eyes are glistening with tears, and sweat is as visible above his upper lip as it was the evening of his first presidential debate with John F. Kennedy in 1960. Richard Nixon stands before members of his administration and White House staff the morning after his resignation on national TV, ready to give his last speech as a politician.[1] The evening before, Nixon's address had been scripted and brief. This one will be extemporaneous and in its ramblings nearly 18 minutes long.

Besides gallows humor, the speech will feature less than genuine self-depreciation, scarred pride, and self-righteous anger. But what will emotionally stand out the most from Nixon's farewell on August 9, 1974 is sadness, with self-pity and anguish joined at the hip. "We'll see you again," Nixon says and winces, before closing his eyes momentarily. Regrets follow. "I should have been by your offices and shaken hands," Nixon says, choking up. Far greater depths of sadness are ahead. "My mother was a saint," Nixon finds himself saying, voice quavering, a tear now taking over his left eye as he recalls her tending to "two boys," two brothers of Nixon's, both "dying of tuberculosis."

Next, an aide brings Nixon the book he requested so everyone can, by implication, hear of another president's fellow misery. That would be Theodore Roosevelt's grief upon losing his wife: "And when my heart's dearest died, the light went from my life forever." This president's own wife, Pat, isn't dead; she's standing nearby. She's not mentioned even once by Nixon, though, as he starts to sniffle, fighting back sobs. By then White House counsel Leonard Garment is, as he later recounts, thinking to himself as he sits in the audience: *Oh, my God, he's beginning to break down. A binge of free association. Money, father, mother, brothers, death. The man is unraveling right before us. He will be the first person to go over the edge on live television.*

Luckily, things never quite reach that point. Sadness can involve a sense of irrevocable loss and is an approach emotion: we long to be hugged and consoled. In August of 1974, however, Nixon is having none of that because sadness is also a submissive emotion, an admission of having been wounded. The essence of sadness is a cry for help, not something Nixon can permit himself. To admit to needing emotional support would go against the line he loves in *Patton* (1970): George C. Scott declaring that "Americans love winners" and "will not tolerate a loser."

A saddened Nixon can't consciously allow himself to feel sad because to do so would mean he's become a loser. So he likewise can't bring himself to directly address losing the presidency. Instead, Nixon pulls himself back from the abyss, tightens his lips in anger and, near the end of his rambling remarks, proclaims: "Always give your best, never get discouraged, never be petty." Further advice that might best apply to Nixon himself follows: "Always remember, others may hate you but those who hate you don't win unless you hate them" (a small smile), "and then you destroy yourself."

Incapable of lightness on that day (everything is going wrong, why *even his watch has stopped working*), Nixon is nevertheless on to something that many people can relate to by denying himself sadness. In America, where we're serenaded with "Don't Worry, Be Happy," sadness can seem embarrassing. In line with *Patton*, it's as if sadness is an emotion we're not supposed to feel. Terms like "sad sack" or being a "downer" put a derogatory spin on an emotion that serves a legitimate purpose in life.

In Pixar's *Inside Out*, a happy, hockey-playing girl from Minnesota is forced to relocate with her family to San Francisco. In the movie, the personified character of Sadness becomes something of a hero given the emotion's redemptive ability to slow us down and help us reflect on, and rectify, what's painful. That's the process Nixon is short-circuiting. Ashamed of feeling weak and vulnerable, he's pretending as if nothing bad has happened as he boards a helicopter after the speech. Standing outside its door, Nixon waves to the people on the South Lawn as if he's just won another campaign.

Spotting Sadness

A sad face *wrinkles* as if its owner is a crumpled piece of paper. Sad people display some of the most obvious emotional clues, including: tears, sobs, and hang-dog looks. Those overt signals aside, sadness can nevertheless also be as subtle as any of the emotions in terms of how it gets displayed. More specifically, sadness appears in seven ways on the face—two of those when it's the only emotion being shown:

Eyes

For about half a second, both eyes close. Due to timing and the use of photos (meaning one doesn't know if fatigue instead of sadness may be the cause), this expression isn't part of my book's data.

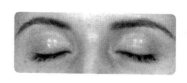

Cheeks

The furrows that angle down and away from the nose nostrils deepen and pull upwards, creating an often very subtle wince. The upper lip simultaneously pulls upward and slightly sideways.

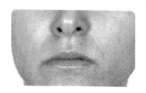

There are another five ways that sadness gets expressed. In each of these cases, one or more of the other core emotions will likewise be shown:

Eyebrows

The inner part of one or both eyebrows lifts upwards, often creating forehead wrinkles.[2]
(sadness, fear, surprise)

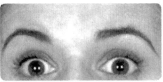

Eyebrows

The eyebrows come together and pull down, creating a vertical crease between the eyebrows.
(sadness, anger, fear)

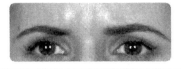

Eyes

Activity around the eyes almost suggests joy. But instead of a twinkle appearing, with sadness the eyes often lose focus.
(sadness, happiness)

Mouth

The corners of the mouth sag.
(sadness, disgust)

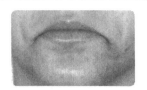

Mouth & Chin

The chin's dimpled skin rises and the mouth forms an upside-down smile.
(sadness, anger, disgust)

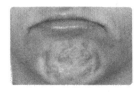

Sadness's Top 10 List

Compared to the dominant, approach emotions of anger and happiness, the *submissive*, approach emotion of sadness is relatively rare (at least in public, the source of the celebrity photographs I had access to for this book). While those two other approach emotions each account for over 30% of the celebrity emoting captured in *Famous Faces Decoded*, the average amount of sadness is a little above 8%. Male celebrities contributing to that average show nearly a third more sadness than their female counterparts. Accordingly, the Top 10 list for Most Sad consists largely of men enduring various degrees of anguish. Hillary Clinton and Janis Joplin are the only two women to appear, both of whom I might note have been derided by their critics as insufficiently feminine.

Most Sad

Donald Trump
Richard Nixon
Hillary Clinton
Marlon Brando
Tiger Woods
Johnny Cash
Janis Joplin
Jay-Z
John McEnroe
Cam Newton

Least Sad

Martha Stewart
Estee Lauder
Sandra Bullock
Joe Montana
Diana Ross
Kate Winslet
Jackie Onassis
Howard Stern
Ellen DeGeneres
Jimmy Page*
Gloria Steinem*
* Two-way tie

Greater male sadness will be surprising to anyone who assumes men so favor anger as a coping mechanism that they're not vulnerable to sadness. The Top 10 list for Least Sad may, likewise, surprise people because it mostly involves females. Donald Trump has said: "Women are much tougher and more calculating than men"; maybe he's right.

Marlon Brando

Voted

happiness
sadness

Actual

sadness
fear

Rare

pleasure

How good are people at spotting sadness? With a detection accuracy rate of 49%, the result for sadness qualifies as merely fourth best among eight options. So it's not surprising that only Tiger Woods, Janis Joplin, and Marlon Brando were correctly seen by voters as having sadness loom large in their emotional make-up. For the other seven celebrities on the Top 10 Most Sad list, the voters were way off the mark. They didn't detect sadness as being *even in the picture* in terms of prevalence, when in fact sadness is very characteristic of all of these celebrities.

Let's start with the good news: a largely correct forecasting example. Marlon Brando's famous brooding performances range from playing Stanley Kowalski in *A Streetcar Named Desire* (1951) to Colonel Walter E. Kurtz in *Apocalypse Now* (1979). Those performances might have helped voters notice Brando's signature (on- and off-screen) expression of eyebrows lowered and knitted together, although they still believed happiness was more his thing. Count this actor in the accurate emotional detection column, however, in that sadness was at least voters' second choice for Brando.

Jay-Z

Voted

happiness
contempt

Actual

sadness
fear

Rare

satisfaction

Now for the bad news in terms of accuracy: in five instances here, the amount of sadness these celebrities express makes that emotion their stand-out result, and yet voters didn't notice. Donald Trump, Richard Nixon, Hillary Clinton, and Johnny Cash were all seriously misjudged, as was Jay-Z. Whether it's sadness expressed by a wrinkle between his eyebrows or a wincing cheek, Jay-Z fights through sorrow. He remains the wistful, contemplative musician who remarked, "I'm hungry for knowledge," on his way to holding the *Billboard* record for the most number one albums by a solo artist: 14 and counting.

What May Cause Sadness

Taken to extremes, sadness becomes depression.[3] In those cases, depressed people will often feel trapped in an adverse past they can't get out of their heads. But even with ordinary sadness, there's a tendency to see the world through a rear-view-mirror perspective, whereby past disappointments can color and limit faith that future situations will turn out well. The following set of seven causes explores the overly strong internal focus that is so much a part of feeling this emotion.

1. We're dealing with rejection, often involving a sense of having been abandoned as part of suffering from isolation.

Back for her 10th high school class reunion, Janis Joplin is asked by a clueless TV interviewer: "Did you entertain in Port Arthur?" (meaning, did she ever sing there in her home town along the Texas coast). "Only when I walked down the aisles," the rock star cackles in response. The reality, however, is much more painful than Joplin is letting on.[4] How can she forget incidents like being named "Ugliest Man on Campus" after escaping Port Arthur for a stop at the University of Texas in Austin?

In the way she bellows, cries, and stamps her feet, Joplin-the-performer can find pleasure, or at least release, from what Joplin-the-person is suffering through. Cheerful, yet melancholy. A white woman singing— maybe the correct verb is *overwhelming*—the blues. Those are among Joplin's many contradictions, all of them hard to sort out. "I can't talk about my singing," she tells an interviewer. "I'm inside it. How can you describe something you're inside of?"

To witness Joplin immersed in performing, watch the video of her squeezing everything she can out of "Piece of My Heart" (1969). In it, she goes from the sad, anxious lifting of her inner eyebrows when the song begins to a fist-pumping, joyful look by the end. Along the way, she's invited members of the audience up on stage. By song's close, Joplin is singing encircled by adoring fans at close range. All the same, she's still only holding a microphone in her arms. That's in keeping with Joplin's signature remark: "Onstage I make love to 25,000 people, then I go home alone."

2. We're dealing with a loss of self-esteem (or even just the prospect of losing it).

For psychologists, the overwhelming verdict is that Donald Trump is the ultimate narcissist.[5] That's a personality disorder the Mayo Clinic calls the mark of fragile self-esteem, noting that those who suffer from narcissism "may be generally unhappy." If true, then what's the cause? Odds are there's no need to look further than Trump's relationship with his dad. The usual culprit for narcissism is parents who aren't affirmative enough, causing the child to long for praise from any source. Given to superlatives, Donald wasn't shy about saying at his father's funeral in 1999 that Fred Trump's greatest achievement was his "fantastic son," namely himself.

Wanting more attention, more approval from his real estate mogul father, while outdoing him, certainly describes Trump to those who have known him well. Abe Wallach, once the head of acquisitions for the Trump Organization, has called Trump "the most insecure man I've ever met," someone who needs to "fill a void inside. He used to do it with deals and sex. Now he does it with publicity."[6] Manic behavior, *yes*. Trump moving on from sex? *Not so much*. Notably lacking the contentment signaled by happiness, Trump admits that "It's the hunt that I believe I love" and so "I just keep pushing." In business, that approach might be justifiable. But in the context of cavorting with adult entertainers or groping other women (which Trump boasted of doing on the *Access Hollywood* tape that emerged during the 2016 campaign), it's as if Trump's deep-seated sadness has crippled his sense of decency and fair play.

3. We're dealing with a loss of praise and social support.

At age 12, Johnny Cash goes off fishing one Saturday while his older brother Jack stays behind, cutting wood to help make money for the family.[7] Using a giant framesaw, Jack loses his balance and gets fatally injured. "I had to take out too many of his insides," the doctor admits to Cash's parents after doing what he could for the boy. For years after Jack's death, Cash's father, Ray, will say: "John, you should be more like your brother. You're lazy, no account [sic], shiftless."

Cash will subsequently wish he died that day. Feeling guilty and sad, he often tells himself: "I want to be more like" my brother Jack "to get my father to finally accept me." In times of trouble, Cash will wonder "What would Jack (an aspiring preacher) do?" and the country music legend's first commercial hit will be the song "Cry, Cry, Cry" (1957).

4. We're dealing with disappointment, often related to high, unrealistic expectations.

In April of 1994, the internet's stunning growth causes Jeff Bezos to quit his job at a New York City hedge fund. "Regret-minimization framework" is how he describes deciding to take the risk.[8] In running Amazon, Bezos is philosophical about setbacks he can't entirely let go of: "I've made billions of dollars of failures at Amazon.com. Literally billions of dollars of failures," he says in an interview, comparing those experiences to "getting a root canal with no anesthesia."

How to explain the man the *Harvard Business Review* has called "The Best-Performing CEO in the World"? How can Bezos both dwell on and yet overcome a litany of costly failures and disappointments? The answer is he plunges onward into many new ventures, some of which pan out big-time. While his biological father used to be in circuses, Bezos qualifies as his own dream machine. The Amazon CEO is still the same guy who, as a high school valedictorian, told *The Miami Herald* his goal in life was "to build space hotels, amusement parks, yachts and colonies" for millions of people orbiting the earth. It's a dream Bezos retains, even at the risk of setting himself up for what could be another, big disappointment by literally aiming so high and far away.

5. We're dealing with physical pain, possibly involving a general loss of health and functionality.

With a track record of locking teachers in rooms, as well as setting fires, Marlon Brando fails high school and is no more accepting of authority figures upon reaching Hollywood. What's behind the pattern?[9] Try a father who beat him, and an alcoholic mother whom a young Brando searched the local bars for many a night in hopes of bringing her home. Those influences will all come together when Brando plays *The Godfather* (1972), a macho, thuggish man turning gentle and sensitive in old age. For Brando, any scenes that require anger inspire memories of "my father hitting me." In contrast, for scenes requiring compassion he calls on memories of the boy whose mother "chose a bottle over caring for me." By mid-life, one of Brando's favorite quotes has become the Jesuit motto: "Give me a child until he is seven and I will give you the man."

6. We're dealing with the loss of a treasured object.

As Tiger Woods gives his press conference apology in early 2010 before a hand-picked audience, he barely shows any emotion. It's as if the script has been ghost-*written* before being ghost-*read* by Woods. When the golfer says he has "bitterly disappointed all of you" seated before him, nobody's home, emotionally speaking. Woods shows no visible sadness, no regret, regarding his affairs with other women. Left unacknowledged, the scandal's moment of greatest drama: Woods crashing his Escalade into a fire hydrant around 2:30 a.m., with his wife Elin allegedly in pursuit.

When does Woods emote during the press conference? Rarely while talking about his wife and kids. Passion kicks in far more when the topic turns to tournament trophies. At the press conference and in subsequent media interviews, Woods winces often—and convincingly—whenever the question concerns getting back on tour to post more golf victories.

7. We're dealing with a sense of hopelessness and helplessness. (But should despair reach the point of feeling worthless, depression has set in.)

According to Nirvana grunge rock star Kurt Cobain, the band's name is from the Buddhist concept of "freedom from pain, suffering and the external world." But what if the pain is mostly internal? In Cobain's suicide note, he doesn't shy away from admitting to sadness or pointing to its likely, original source: his parents' divorce. "There's good in all of us and I think I simply love people too much, so much that it makes me feel too fucking sad. The sad little sensitive, unappreciated, Pisces, Jesus man," he writes, taking a gibe at himself. Loathing and self-loathing intermingle. "Since the age of seven, I've become hateful towards all humans in general," Cobain confesses before adding, "Only because it seems so easy for people to get along and have empathy."

Age seven was two years before Cobain's parents divorced, but storm clouds were probably already gathering in their relationship. The suicide note's divorce reference builds on a 1993 interview[10] in which Cobain recalls turning defiant and withdrawn after his parents' divorce because "I desperately wanted to have the classic, you know, typical family. Mother, father. I wanted that security, so I resented my parents for quite a few years." With no band as of yet, one of Cobain's favorite boyhood activities had been repeatedly drawing the character "Creature from the Black Lagoon" to express—and distance—himself from his own misery.

Four Forms of Sadness

Besides the ordinary version of rain, there's freezing drizzle as well as "snain": a rain/snow mix. Why, there are even sun showers. So it follows that there can't be only one form of sadness, and there isn't.

The first two forms, Deflated and Shaken, signal feeling needy and thrown off-balance in ways that challenge one's sense of being a worthwhile person. In addition to sadness, Deflated can also involve fear more so than surprise. That form is very much about low-grade suffering and anxiety. Despondent people feeling Deflated are probably more likely to slow down. But they may, instead, cope by engaging in a flurry of activity to "paper over" their discomfort. Then with Shaken, surprise gets favored over fear in being yoked to sadness. This second form is more about a set-back leaving a forlorn and rattled person yearning for relief.

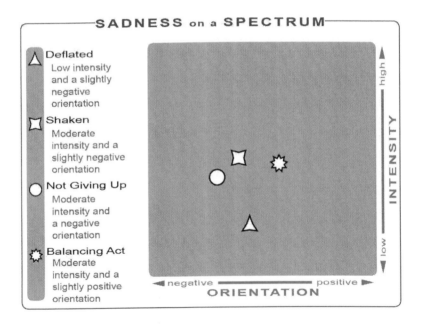

In contrast, the other two forms of sadness, Not Giving Up and Balancing Act, draw on either disgust and anger, or happiness—and thereby demonstrate resiliency. In regards to Not Giving Up, a feeling of loss gets challenged by the intervening influence of anger and disgust. Finally, with Balancing Act the inherent call for help that sadness involves has now been answered by a reason for happiness to enter the picture.

More specifically, each form of sadness gets shown as follows:

Deflated: The single most clear-cut way people exhibit sadness is when the cheeks rise, sometimes just slightly, producing wrinkles from the edge of the nostrils down to the top, outer corners of the lips. This wincing movement also pushes up the skin below the eyes so that they narrow at the corners. When this look is combined with the inner eyebrows rising (instead of pinched together, as they are here), then you're typically moving from what might be sadness merely hinted at, to a more fundamental desire to escape suffering.

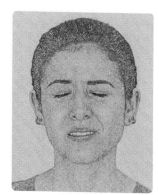

Deflated

Shaken: A cheek-raising wince, combined with a mouth falling open with surprise, reveals people caught off-guard. They're freshly vulnerable to discouragement. Given their shock on feeling sadness, these people look like the equivalent of someone who's just tripped during a walk, landing on the pavement in pain. The accompanying photo adds to this look an ever-so-slightly raised left outer eyebrow.

Not Giving Up: A rodeo clown's painted face showcases a frown. But with a real frown, not only will

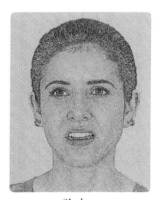

Shaken

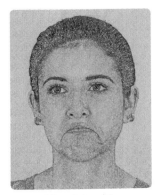

Not giving Up

the lip corners sag; the skin below them simultaneously pouches. Add in an upward chin thrust that puckers the chin and lifts the lower lip, and you've got an upside-down smile—as dramatically shown in the accompanying photo. These sad smiles mix in anger and disgust, creating a resolute flavor. Think in terms of sadness, but not resignation; of disappointment that can and will be recovered from. You can likewise think of this look as showing a determination to "get my life back" to where it was previously.

Balancing Act: Happiness and sadness are opposites that often blend together. The smile on display here is rueful, a coping mechanism. We benefit from sadness when the emotion helps enrich our understanding of a loss, including how we might best recover. At other times, sadness helps us anticipate a disappointment and prepare for the hurt. Sadness combined with offsetting amounts of happiness, however, can be even better, ensuring we extract the benefits of sadness without giving in to that feeling.

Balancing Act

Each Form's Top 10 List

How do sadness's four forms apply to the celebrities facially coded for this book? The two forms that involve more intensely negative reactions—Deflated and Shaken—are heavily represented by politicians (Donald Trump and Hillary Clinton, in particular) as well as by musicians and athletes. With the other two, more resilient forms of sadness, athletes dominate. Besides Trump and Hillary Clinton, additional repeat appearances across these next four Top 10 lists include: Bill Clinton, Janis Joplin, Peyton Manning, Mary Lou Retton, and Venus Williams. When it comes to sadness and these lists, women have a notably strong presence in the realms of music and sports.

Deflated: Donald Trump's supporters believe that his empathy for the challenges many of them face means he will truly "drain the swamp" in the nation's capitol. Detractors insist that "Make America Great Again" says more about his ego than anything else, and that any sadness Trump feels involves self-pity rather than concern for others. What both sides would agree on is that with its apocalyptic language about an "American carnage," Trump's inaugural address was a grim departure from most new presidents' more uplifting remarks.

TOP 10

Deflated
Humphrey Bogart
Donald Trump
Janis Joplin
Hillary Clinton
Peyton Manning
Larry Page
Cam Newton
Larry Ellison
Woody Allen
Jeff Bezos

Besides Trump, others on the Top 10 list for Deflated who may override sadness with a flurry of activity include the entrepreneurial, high-tech trio of Larry Page, Larry Ellison, and Jeff Bezos. Then there's Woody Allen, who has said of his more than 50 movies: "I would erase all but a few."[11] High self-expectations, if not always met, can be one source of sadness. Humphrey Bogart and Janis Joplin also appear here, sharing the fate that they both in their own way struggled for affirmation. In Bogart's case, the actor unsuccessfully sought affection from his taciturn parents while growing up. In Joplin's case, outside of her family she never did find much acceptance in her home town or even Texas at large.

Shaken: Very representative of this form of sadness is the Man in Black: Johnny Cash. Besides the premature loss of his brother Jack, the other most devastating loss in the country music star's life was when his wife died.[12] Day after day, Cash would sit in his wheelchair by June Carter Cash's bed as she lay gravely ill, begging her not to leave him. Then after her death, there was additional rearview-mirror behavior. Not only did Cash pay an artist to paint June's face on the elevator doors of his office, he would also often try to phone her.

Shaken

Donald Trump
John McEnroe
Hillary Clinton
Serena Williams
Mary Lou Retton
Elton John
Johnny Cash
Adele
Janis Joplin
Bill Clinton

Headlining the Top 10 list for Shaken, you'll find Donald Trump and John McEnroe. Both men are notoriously thin-skinned, befitting the theory that a cause of sadness can be the absence of enough praise (or success) to bolster one's self-esteem. In contrast, three celebrities on this list have experienced another cause of sadness: the irrevocable loss of somebody important to them. Removed through death or separation early in their lives was Jack in Cash's case, and the fathers of, respectively, both Adele and Bill Clinton.

Not Giving Up

Barack Obama
Aaron Rodgers
Andy Warhol
Jeb Bush
Bill Clinton
Peyton Manning
Tom Brady
Ted Williams
Roger Clemens
Venus Williams

Not Giving Up: "Sooner or later" Elon Musk has proclaimed, "we must expand life beyond this green and blue ball—or go extinct." His goal is to establish a Mars colony within the next generation and ensure the people living there can use electric transportation.[13] (After all, the atmosphere on Mars lacks the oxygen ordinary cars require.) Given his company's electric cars, how nicely that plan suits the agenda of the CEO of both Tesla Motors and SpaceX. Or so a cynic might say. But you have to hand it to Musk for his never-say-die spirit. Spat on by a disbelieving Russian space designer when he first began to conceptualize a "Mars Oasis," about the only serious things Musk has ever quit on were his first two marriages.

At #11, Musk just barely misses the Top 10 list for Not Giving Up. Those on this list are all world-class athletes or politicians with a single exception: Andy Warhol. As a boy, that artist suffered from a nervous system disease known as St. Vitus' Dance and became a frequently bedridden hypochondriac who, like Musk, was an outcast at school.

Balancing Act: Music and her own bruised self-esteem went together for Mariah Carey from the start. Why, even her first name derives from the plaintive song "They Call the Wind Maria," from the 1951 Broadway musical *Paint Your Wagon*. After her parents' divorce, a youthful Carey would find solace in singing along to music on the radio at night. From such salvation, her career was born.

Other celebrities in the Top 10 list for Balancing Act include: Ringo Starr, whose first drum was a gift the often hospitalized boy latched onto; and the Muppets creator Jim Henson, surely the Walt Disney of his era. In helping to establish *Sesame Street* in 1969, Henson was

TOP 10

Balancing Act

Mary Lou Retton
Charles Schulz
John F. Kennedy
Diane Keaton
Ringo Starr
Janis Joplin
Venus Williams
Whitney Houston
Mariah Carey
Jim Henson

affectionately described by a colleague as having a "whim of steel." Henson's most famous character is alter-ego Kermit the Frog. A good, stable blend of happiness and sadness himself, Kermit sometimes expresses melancholy but is most famous for an open, red mouth that resembles a Valentine whenever he smiles big-time.

Summary

Some people may think that rich-and-famous celebrities are too wealthy to ever feel worthless and sad, but of course that's not true. Charlie Chaplin could still convincingly play his character The Tramp, with the Tramp's wincing smiles, long after the actor had achieved fame and fortune. While nobody supposedly knows you when you're down and out, everybody knows what it's like to feel beaten down at times. We also all instinctively know the sadness look: the frowning, "long" face that comes from feeling blue.

Grief can overwhelm us, and misery can make us literally groan in agony. Even less intense versions of sadness can make us want to hide. Ashamed of feeling weak and vulnerable, we often pretend as if nothing bad has happened. With sadness, every facial muscle movement, subtle or otherwise, serves a greater purpose. It signals our need for help as we seek the support required to persevere and prosper. How else does sadness help us? For one thing, it releases hormones that help foster empathy and compassion. For another, it aids in reflection by slowing us down so that we don't rashly jump into another disaster. Accordingly, sadness can lead to being very good at attending to the small details that might make a big difference at times. Finally, when "down", remember: so close and *yet so far* is the distance between sadness and happiness, as the same lips turned down in a frown will, in rising, offer a smile.

Personality insights revealed by
facial coding comparisons

John F. Kennedy		
Voted	Actual	Rare
happiness	satisfaction	surprise
surprise	sadness	

Robert F. Kennedy		
Voted	Actual	Rare
happiness	sadness	contempt
happiness	acceptance	

Voters saw the two brothers as upbeat, especially Robert Kennedy, though in reality sadness also filled them both. What separates them emotionally is what they didn't feel very often. A rarely surprised John Kennedy contrasts with a rarely contemptuous Bobby, who of the two was younger, smaller, and quite possibly more empathetic. Bobby grew "not by reading books, as brother Jack had." Instead, "experience transformed him," Larry Tye writes,[1] in praising Bobby's 1968 campaign for its spontaneity. For example, the candidate won over a crowd in Nebraska by ad-libbing, "There goes my farm program" when the wind blew away the pages of his prepared speech, leading to a rousing, improvisational, from-the-heart address.

Serena Williams		
Voted	Actual	Rare
happiness	disgust	*joy*
anger	contempt	

Venus Williams		
Voted	Actual	Rare
happiness	*joy*	contempt
surprise	sadness	

Voters saw both tennis stars as mildly happy. In fact, Serena Williams's perceived anger is often actually disgust and Venus Williams's mild happiness deserves to be upgraded to joy. Those two corrections aside, the big difference between the two sisters is Venus's tender sadness versus Serena's contempt—a sign of superiority you could say Serena has earned. In 1992, when the sisters were both still tennis juniors, their father, Richard, said[2] that Venus would be a champion, but Serena is "like a pit-bull dog. Once she gets ahold of you she won't let go." Then he rightly predicted that "Serena will probably be a better player than Venus," despite excellence from both.

Voted	Actual	Rare
surprise	fear	anger
happiness	*joy*	

Voted	Actual	Rare
sadness	surprise	anger
fear	fear	

Voters saw emotional darkness in Michael Jackson, versus a sunnier picture of his sister. Granted, Janet Jackson is more capable of happiness than Michael was. But what the siblings have in common is fear, which makes sense given how their dad behaved. In Michael's autobiography, *Moonwalk*, he remembers how Joe, his father, would critique the family rehearsals in Gary, Indiana: "If you messed up, you got hit, sometimes with a belt, sometimes with a switch."[3] And yet well into adulthood the "King of Pop" (who could move backwards while seemingly walking forward) still lived with his parents, believing, "Oh, no. I think I'd die on my own. I'd be so lonely."

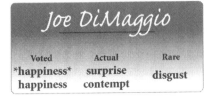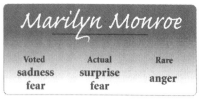

Voted	Actual	Rare
happiness	surprise	disgust
happiness	contempt	

Voted	Actual	Rare
sadness	surprise	anger
fear	fear	

Newly retired from the New York Yankees, Joe DiMaggio saw some publicity shots of Marilyn Monroe and asked her for a date. Their brief marriage ended abruptly. After Monroe filmed the skirt-flying subway grate scene in Manhattan for *The Seven Year Itch* (1955), DiMaggio beat her and she left him. Were they hopelessly mismatched? Shared surprise aside, the signs weren't good. The voters were off-base to see DiMaggio as happy. A smirk isn't a smile. The slugger's contempt and Monroe's fear couldn't have been a very good dynamic. Most likely the more she was anxious, the more he would have disrespected her for feeling ill at ease.

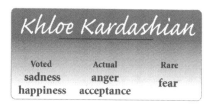

Voters perceived differences between the three sisters. They judged Kim Kardashian-West the most upbeat, Kourtney Kardashian somewhere in between, and Khloe Kardashian the least cheerful. Yes, Kim and Kourtney both show mild happiness. Anger rather than sadness best defines Khloe, however, while Kim stands out for showing contempt.

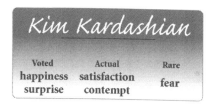

What none of the three feel is much fear, which figures. The title of *Keeping Up with the Kardhasians* updates the cliché, "keeping up with the Joneses," the first family in Newport, Rhode Island to build a Guilded Era mansion. Nowadays, put cameras in a California mansion and, voilá, the secure, privileged lifestyle the Jones' dinner guests witnessed in person has become what the Kardashian viewers see on TV.

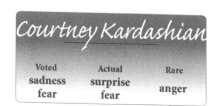

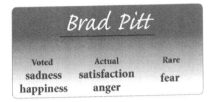

Having left one woman (Jennifer Aniston) and having been left by the other woman here (Angelina Jolie), the interesting question becomes: was Brad Pitt emotionally well matched with either one? Voters saw Aniston and Pitt as more compatible based on their sharing mild happiness. But someone close to Pitt has said of Jolie: Pitt saw "a very adventurous person who was grabbing onto life,"[4] which he preferred.

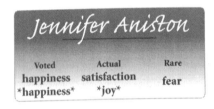

Indeed, Jolie and Pitt share an affinity for the aggressive emotion of anger, versus Aniston's sunnier disposition. The intriguing result is that despite her reputation for being somewhat neurotic, the one argument in favor of Aniston being better suited for Pitt is that they both rarely show fear.

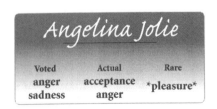

Bill Clinton		
Voted	**Actual**	**Rare**
surprise happiness	sadness disgust	acceptance

Hillary Clinton		
Voted	**Actual**	**Rare**
happiness anger	sadness contempt	acceptance

At the 2016 Democratic Convention, Bill Clinton certainly did his best to shape the Clintons' relationship as a romantic fairy tale that began with boy-meets-girl on a college campus. In truth it's been a tumultuous marriage, with both the couple's closeness as well as their venting evident for their staffs to witness. While voters saw this couple as sympatico in sharing mild happiness, closer to reality is mutual sadness. Then add disgust for Bill and contempt for Hillary Clinton, and harsher feelings enter the picture. Who can be tougher to handle? Former White House Chief of Staff Leon Panetta[5] recalls this difference between the couple: while Bill "could be a screamer, too," Hillary's temper when feeling sadly let down by aides "had much more sustained velocity, for a longer period of time."

George H. W. Bush		
Voted	**Actual**	**Rare**
happiness surprise	fear sadness	satisfaction

George W. Bush		
Voted	**Actual**	**Rare**
happiness surprise	fear contempt	satisfaction

Voters saw no difference between father and son, despite there being some emotional daylight between them. Sadness helps to define George H. W. Bush, who's a worrier. Critics would say that George W. Bush should have been more concerned in office himself, rather than declare "Mission Accomplished" in Iraq. At the 2004 Republican convention, George W. said: "Some folks look at me and see a certain swagger—which in Texas is called walking." George W. also taunted Iraqi insurgents by telling them to "Bring it on." Self-confident contempt defines George W. to a degree not true of his polite, more self-effacing dad.

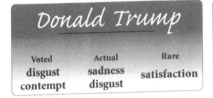

Donald Trump			Ivanka Trump		
Voted	Actual	Rare	Voted	Actual	Rare
disgust contempt	sadness disgust	satisfaction	contempt happiness	disgust contempt	sadness

More emotionally buttoned-up than her dad (which isn't hard to do, given his style), Ivanka Trump stands out for emotional displays centered around the spurning emotions of disgust and contempt. Disgust is a feeling Donald Trump and his daughter share. But to see an occasion of them not on the same page, watch the 2013 *Wendy Williams Show* episode[6] in which they're asked what they have in common. "Either real estate or golf," Ivanka says. Then she reveals intense disgust and fear, followed by a sort of baffled, masking smile. That's because Donald, pointing at her, has instead answered with a grin, "Well, I was going to say sex, but I can't relate that to her."

Beyonce			Jay-Z		
Voted	Actual	Rare	Voted	Actual	Rare
happiness happiness	*joy* acceptance	contempt	*happiness* contempt	sadness fear	satisfaction

Music's royal couple makes it work,[7] despite vastly different upbringings and emotional displays. Aided by attending first an elementary school and then a high school devoted to the fine arts, Beyonce was already on her way to selling 60 million records as a member of the group Destiny's Child by the time she was 16 years of age. Voters see Beyonce as happy, and she is. Try as he might, Jay-Z can't escape emotional scars. Raised in the projects in Brooklyn, he began selling crack on the streets at age twelve. Sure, he smiles some—but not much. Satisfaction is rarely felt. Jay-Z shows sadness and fear instead of the self-confident contempt that voters saw in him. He's down, she's up, and together recent troubles in their marriage have resulted in some of their best solo work ever.

part  two

spurning

emotions

Contempt

Cool or Cruel?

What Contempt Means

The year 2005 will forever loom large in Tom Cruise's life. In April, he begins dating the actress Katie Holmes in a romance the media quickly dubs "TomKat". The following month, Cruise madly jumps around atop a couch on *The Oprah Winfrey Show* while declaring his newfound love for Holmes. Then in November, Cruise marries Holmes in a Church of Scientology ceremony held in Italy. Besides wedding vows, the actor is thereby affirming his faith that a galactic emperor named Xenu sent frozen souls to earth to inhabit human bodies.[1]

Scientology also happens to blame psychiatry for condoning the use of drugs prescribed for treatment. So three days after the couch jump, Cruise publicly criticizes Brooke Shields for using Paxil to cope with her postpartum depression, causing Shields, in turn, to tell Cruise to "stick to saving the world from aliens."

Happy to milk the controversy, Matt Lauer of NBC's *The Today Show* now invites Cruise to give an interview.[2] During it, Cruise promptly criticizes Shields again for her use of medication rather than something like vitamins to cure her depression. Yes, Cruise tries to walk the criticism back a little by saying, "I really care about Brooke Shields." But then he states, "I know that psychiatry is … is a pseudo science."

Lauer's various attempts to get Cruise to tolerate the kind of treatment plan that worked for Shields finally leads Cruise to sputter aloud, "Matt, Matt, Matt, you don't even—*you're glib*. You don't even know what Ritalin is." To stress his point, Cruise jabs his finger at Lauer at the same time that his upper lip is repeatedly curling in contempt.

A full three years later, Cruise will semi-apologize: "I came across as arrogant. That's not who I am." Well, maybe; but there's no denying what viewers saw that day. Cruise was clearly dismissing Lauer's attempts to find some middle ground, and in doing so feeling contempt: an emotion about relishing one's superiority to others.

From the introduction to *Famous Faces Decoded*—namely, the Nature and Frequency of Emotions chart—you already know the score. Contempt is a dominant as opposed to submissive emotion. But likewise consider the flavor of this emotion: you're basically *annointing* yourself as someone worthy of exaltation. The essence of contempt is almighty spurning. If you're feeling smug, you feel like you're riding high. You've found other people and circumstances unworthy, meaning you can freely disregard them as beneath you. Given a desire to simultaneously keep away from what's been tainted by mediocrity, contempt also qualifies as an avoidance rather than an approach emotion. While happiness means you're a "hugger", with contempt you believe you're better than others. So you're excluding people, rather than embracing them.

The standard definition of contempt is that this emotion consists of a cross between anger and disgust. But left out, and sorely needed in order to fully grasp contempt, is a degree of happiness.[3] Think of the old cartoon character Snidely Whiplash and his evil smile as contempt personified.

The upside of contempt is that it serves as an expression of self-assurance. You're happy going negative. In judging others, you condescendingly conclude that you know best. The downside is that unwarranted contempt can rob you of the benefit of collaborating with others. Feeling contempt makes it hard to get along well with anyone tagged as deficient. The all-too-human urge to see ourselves as superior is a by-product, if not the linchpin, of hierarchies ranging from England's and India's respective class and caste systems, to a company's organizational chart.

Spotting Contempt

A contemptuous face *smirks* as if that person is giving you a mocking salute. These smirks are mostly unilateral, occurring on just one side of a person's face. More specifically, there's only a pair of ways in which contempt gets shown. The first applies to contempt only, and the second involves two other emotions as well:

Mouth

A lip corner will tighten and often rise a little, pulling the skin slightly inward while also narrowing that lip corner. A wrinkle or bulge will form at that same lip corner and may create a small dimple or cavity in the cheek.

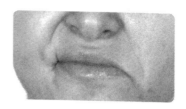

Cheeks & Mouth

If only one side of the top lip is curling upwards, causing the nostril above it to flare and the skin to pouch along that side of the nose, then it's a clear sign of contempt. In this photo, the asymmetry is so subtle that, overall, there's anger, disgust, and just a dose of contempt.

(contempt, anger, disgust)

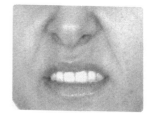

Contempt's Top 10 List

Contempt is a comparatively rare emotion but often toxic when it does appear. In *Blink: The Power of Thinking Without Thinking*, Malcolm Gladwell visits the Love Lab at the University of Washington. The lab utilizes facial coding for marriage counseling and has found that nothing is more accurate in predicting a couple's eventual divorce than strong feelings of contempt for one another. With merely 15 minutes of coded videotape per couple, the accuracy rate linking emotions like contempt to divorce can reach 90%.[4]

Most Contempt

Bill Gates
Aaron Rodgers
Neil Armstrong
J. K. Rowling
David Letterman
Tom Brady
Barack Obama
Cam Newton
Hillary Clinton
Hank Aaron

Least Contempt

James Dean
Martha Stewart
Princess Diana
Robert Redford
George Harrison
Leonardo DiCaprio
Diana Ross
Jim Henson
Mickey Mantle
Tom Hanks*
Charles Schulz*
*two-way tie

Among the celebrities analyzed for *Famous Faces Decoded*, on average only 3% of their emoting involves contempt. Think of contempt as the opposite of a diamond wedding ring. Both come in small packages. The difference? While a diamond ring represents a big gift, contempt can create big problems.

Of further note is that except for the weakest level of happiness, namely acceptance, no other emotional state exhibits a larger gender split than contempt does. Male celebrities in this book are, as a group, almost twice as likely to reveal contempt as their female counterparts, with the Top 10 list for Most Contempt full of cocky male athletes.

Turning to the Top 10 list for Least Contempt, what do we find? Mickey Mantle aside, athletes are absent. Instead, two visual artists appear: the Muppets creator Jim Henson, and the *Peanuts* cartoonist Charles Schulz. Also gracing the list is the "People's Princess": Diana, Princess of Wales. The opposite of aloof, she physically touched and emotionally comforted those suffering from leprosy and AIDS. When her cause then became clearing land mines, Princess Diana traveled to Angola. There she obligingly walked through a field of mines—twice—ensuring more publicity, because some of the paparazzi hadn't caught her first effort on camera.[5]

How good are people at spotting contempt? Pretty poor, for at 21% contempt is the emotion voters were third worst at detecting accurately. (Only the scores for disgust and fear are lower.) Correct examples of voters linking this emotion to the celebrities in the Top 10 Most Contempt list don't exist. However, there are two semi-correct answers along with eight instances where contempt wasn't on voters' radar screen *at all*.

What are the two semi-correct answers? They involve a pair of quarterbacks, the Green Bay Packers' Aaron Rodgers and the Carolina Panthers' Cam Newton, and two alternative blends of emotions that together can help to define contempt. The first blend is disgust and happiness. That's the upbeat, self-confident version of contempt that Rogers exemplifies. The other is the traditional blend of emotions used by psychologists to define contempt, namely, anger and disgust—which is what voters chose in describing Newton's most characteristic emotions. So at least voters were

Aaron Rodgers

Voted

happiness disgust

Actual

contempt disgust

Rare

joy

in the right vicinity for both men, even if they failed to label the two star quarterbacks as highly prone to contempt.

Now it's time for one of the eight complete misses. Consider Microsoft cofounder Bill Gates. A post on Yahoo Answers parallels voters' misidentification of one of the world's richest people as simply a happy camper. The individual who's posting wonders aloud: "I once read a book, and it briefly said Bill Gate [sic] was an arrogant person. Is he really an arrogant person in real life? He doesn't look like it (at least from his physical appearance)."

Bill Gates

Voted

happiness *happiness*

Actual

contempt satisfaction

Rare

fear

Such can be the fine line between a smile and a smirk, or a combination thereof. With Gates, notice how often his smile is accompanied by the upwardly-angled, dimpling of a lip corner: contempt's tell-tale mark.

What May Cause Contempt

In deciding whether contempt is a cool or cruel emotion, consider the positive meanings of "cool": qualities like staying calm or being socially hip. Feeling smug can feel nice. But when the definition of cool moves to *not* showing much interest in, nor affection for, others a cool, slightly cold emotion can become downright mean. So in the end, the answer is that contempt is both cool and cruel. The emotion's range of nuances will become clearer from this set of six likely causes of contempt.

1. Our faith in behaving properly ensures that when violations occur, our instinct is to pull back from anyone perceived as breaking the rules.

Why does Neil Armstrong get chosen to be the first person to walk on the moon in 1969? Part of the answer is his sense of decorum, anchored by not having a big ego.[6] NASA officials don't have to worry that fame will go to his head. Proof that NASA chose well is a story about a woman coming up to Armstrong on a putting green years later and asking him, "Are you somebody that I should know?" Armstrong's reply: "Probably not." In the astronaut's case, humility counter-intuitively leads to good-natured scorn for behavior he doesn't condone.

Another story brings that point home. In this case, Armstrong is on a golf course in 2002 with Clint Eastwood so that the two men can discuss a possible movie about NASA and Armstrong's experiences. A strong sense of honor means that sooner than later, however, Armstrong takes his bag of clubs off Eastwood's cart and walks away. The two men have irreconcilable viewpoints about the new movie idea. Eastwood's prior release, *Space Cowboys* (2000), had involved lots of free-wheeling behavior by U.S. Air Force pilots. Armstrong believes Eastwood has still got it all wrong. The prospective movie won't be any more honest—and therefore not worth making—because it would again fail to emphasize careful, engineering-based procedures over wild, colorful personalities.

2. We regard another person or group of people as inferior, meaning any act of exclusion or correction is for everyone's good.

The code of conduct for the regrettably few, big-time female politicians in America is fraught with assumptions about how a woman "should" behave. Add in how any candidate handles an election defeat, and the standard for female leaders becomes even more difficult.

In a Portsmouth, New Hampshire coffee house in January of 2008, Hillary Clinton gets asked by one of the 15 women gathered there how she does it, how she finds the fortitude to get up and hit the campaign trail day after day. "It's not easy, it's not easy," Clinton initially says, shaking her head. Her eyes are watery long before she finishes her answer. Clinton has just come in third, behind Barack Obama and John Edwards in Iowa's caucus voting among Democrats. It was a crushing defeat that now leads to a softening of her robotic (and surely often sexist) "Ice Queen" image.

At a campaign event later the same day as the Portsmouth coffee house get-together, Clinton lingers on stage, takes every question, and for once doesn't show any contempt. It's this more emotionally open version of Clinton that aids her win in the New Hampshire primary the following Tuesday, after having been far down in the polls.

Fast forward to 2017, and how has Clinton handled losing to Donald Trump? Many people would say not so well,[7] based on Clinton's re-emergence 100 days into Trump's presidency to begin a flurry of appearances. At a Women for Women International luncheon, she smirks while talking about potential supporters who "got scared off" by late-breaking events during the campaign. Is it James Comey, Julian Assange, or voters lacking backbone who trigger such contempt? Or all of the above, and more? (When asked as part of a *New Yorker* profile if she stands by her remark that a larger number of Trump's backers were "irredeemable" and a "basket of deplorables," Clinton bypasses the opportunity to be generous and instead declares: "I don't take back the description.")

Clinton likewise often smirks on stage at a 2017 Code Conference. There, she discusses everything from the digital voter files she received from the Democratic National Committee ("poor, nonexistent, wrong"), to lucrative speeches for Goldman Sachs defended anew ("they paid me"). Quickly, a consensus has emerged regarding those events and Clinton's memoir, *What Happened.* That consensus paints the former candidate as more derisive and defensive, rather than reflective, about accepting her role in losing the election.

3. We consider the actions of others to be amoral transgressions, and so we become filled with distrust.

After having been promised artistic freedom when he signs up (as a teenager) with Warner Brothers in 1977, Prince has by 1993 had enough. Now he appears in public with the word "slave" across one cheek and a sneer at the corner of his mouth, ready to change his name to an unpronounceable "Love Symbol." The impetus for these anti-corporate moves is Prince's sense of having been commercially exploited. He isn't alone. Other musicians also often feel that way about their record labels, but typically don't have the means to fight back. Another motivation for Prince's rebellion arises—even more profoundly—from African-Americans' history of enslavement. As the rock star observes: "I don't own Prince's music. If you don't own your masters, your master owns you."[8]

4. Our confidence in being superior leads us to assert power and status.

It's often said that a company's culture starts at the top. So when a reporter covering Microsoft's anti-trust case in 1999 hears a senior aide to Bill Gates rant about "sub-50-IQ people" wrongly daring to question the company's business practices,[9] you've got to question, in turn, Gates's influence. By then, Gates is already well known for an imperial management style exemplified by his interrupting managers' presentations with comments like, "That's the stupidest thing I've ever heard!" and "Why don't you just give up your options and join the Peace Corps?" Certainly, the judge presiding over the anti-trust case isn't enamored of Gates (and may be rather smug himself). Afterwards, this judge says of Microsoft's CEO: "I think he has a Napoleonic concept of himself and his company, an arrogance that derives from power and unalloyed success."[10] (Over the years following the anti-trust suit, the beneficent efforts of the Bill & Melinda Gates Foundation will improve Bill's image, but his smirking doesn't go away.)

5. We've been deeply hurt or insulted by somebody and, as tolerance shrivels, we either take revenge or disengage from others.

J. K. Rowling is 14 years old when she discovers her life-long heroine. That would be the author Jessica Mitford, who headed to Spain during that country's Civil War to fight against fascism. Later in life,[11] Rowling will describe Mitford as someone who "liked nothing better than a good fight, preferably against a pompous and hypocritical target." Cast in similar terms will be Rowling's famous young wizard. How fitting that Harry Potter's destiny is to fight Lord Voldemort, a character whom Rowling has described as a "raging psychopath," without remorse, who believes he's superior to everyone else.

Rowling's childhood unfolded in a home with an ill mom and a dad who frightened her. Not "particularly happy" growing up, Rowling has compared living with her parents to the Stockholm syndrome: you're a hostage who must "make friends with the warders."

Nowadays, Rowling's oppressors are members of the media. Their incessant questions often get greeted by the defensive barrier of a raised upper lip and a jeering twist of the author's mouth. Some 50 times Rowling has taken legal action against the press to protect her privacy. That her publisher has developed the practice of "denial marketing," whereby the "more people want, the less you give," suits Rowling's outlook perfectly well. Rowling's husband, Neil Murray, certainly knows the score. Murray admits that when his wife is "very stressed, she'll detach herself and only trust one person, and that's herself."[12]

6. We reject others, finding them unworthy of our attention (thereby eliminating the need for us to engage with them).

When Barack Obama bursts upon America's political stage, his message of hope and kindly, joyful smiles predominate. But with the 2008 Pennsylvania primary looming, Obama has become the front-runner and now Hillary Clinton and the press are targeting him. In a Philadelphia debate, a gotcha question makes Obama tilt his head back, scoff, and literally look down his nose at the media panelists, revealing a desire to avoid the stench-in-the-trench of politics. Given his simultaneous desire—to run the country—could being aloof limit Obama's effectiveness as a leader?

In office, Obama won't stroke the egos of members of Congress to ensure legislation gets passed. Selling is a task he delegates to Joe Biden and staff.[13] Obama prefers staying true to his 2008 inaugural speech, with its call to resist "pettiness and immaturity" (even as some opponents rely on less dignified tactics). As a result, the President gets characterized by his White House advisors as preferring to play "chess in a town full of checkers players" because he's a decent guy who would "rather be right than win."[14]

Four Forms of Contempt

Why might contempt be such a hard emotion for a marriage to survive? In essence, how the face displays this emotion matches up well with an instinct to move up and away from the object of derision. Contempt differs from the other emotions in *Famous Faces Decoded* by being a case where those who feel it aren't as likely to be in "the throes" of an emotion (like raging anger, trembling fear, or blissed-out happiness). Instead, they're people for whom an attitude toward someone or something has crystallized, only to be now re-activated in response to a new event. So regardless of which form pertains, the intensity levels are always moderate.

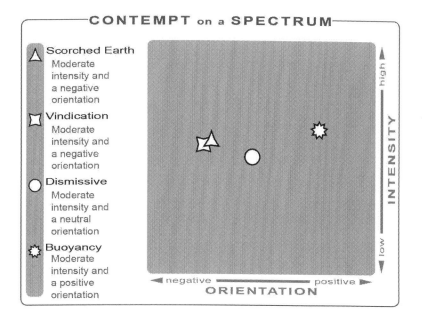

CONTEMPT on a SPECTRUM

Scorched Earth
Moderate intensity and a negative orientation

Vindication
Moderate intensity and a negative orientation

Dismissive
Moderate intensity and a neutral orientation

Buoyancy
Moderate intensity and a positive orientation

INTENSITY — high / low

ORIENTATION — ◄ negative — positive ►

Of these four forms of contempt, the first two, Scorched Earth and Vindication, are decidedly negative, combining corrosive contempt with either vengeful anger or disappointed sadness. By adding different levels of happiness, the other two forms, Dismissive and Buoyancy, range from conveying modest, self-contained assurance to the outright enjoyment that comes from believing you've achieved supremacy. What unites all four of these forms? It's that with contempt the themes of distrust and disrespect are forever in play.

More specifically, each form of contempt gets shown as follows:

Scorched Earth: Since contempt is usually defined as a mixture of disgust and anger, Scorched Earth qualifies as contempt on steroids. With this form, throw in an extra dollop of anger because of an eyes-narrowed glare or lips pressed firmly together. The result is a hard, high-pressured look like the one evident here. Notice the bulge beneath the lower lip. Frequently, the contemptuous person's anger arises from feeling betrayed. People haven't been meritorious, despite their promises. So anger reflects a desire to take control of the situation by using scorn to punish those people for not being true to their word.

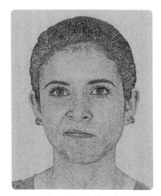

Scorched Earth

Given its air of self-righteous indignation, Scorched Earth equates to *you let me down, how dare you!* The subsequent behavior doesn't have to be spiteful, however. By analogy, a constructive use of this feeling is akin to the way forest fires can enable new growth. Burned vegetation fertilizes the soil and new plants emerge, thanks to more sunlight reaching the forest floor. Yes, scorn can clear the way for rejuvenation.

Vindication: A second form of contempt involves people expressing sadness. They might be unhappy that so-and-so can't, in their estimation, be trusted enough to bother with. Or they might feel isolated and lonely, suspecting that somebody close to them isn't a capable ally. A feeling of Vindication means the disdainful person's doubts have proven to be justified. Therefore, Vindication becomes a consolation prize. While

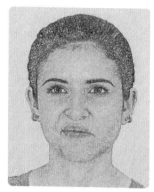

Vindication

it would have been better not to have found shortcomings in the other party, at least you can still regard yourself as being perfectly fine.

With sad contempt, a frown or wince accompanies the usual signs of scorn. In the photo shown here, the falling right corner of the mouth signals dejection most clearly. Since sadness is part of the mix, the spirit of Vindication could be summarized as a matter of *you let me down, leaving me feeling disappointed and wishing you could do better.* Bitter chagrin rules the day. The upside is that this form of contempt can be powered by a strong desire to ensure justice gets served.

Dismissive: Welcome to partly-sunny contempt as mild happiness enters the picture. Rather than *sneering,* think in terms of *snickering.* This more upbeat feeling may come from the disdainful person concluding that others can be safely disregarded. Then again, the happiness involved may signal relief—even liberation from—the need to interact with

Dismissive

someone never quite welcome in the first place. Whatever the cause, the usual signs of contempt go well with satisfaction or acceptance smiles. Note both the model's unilaterally raised lip and smirk, plus the hint of a grin. The spirit of being Dismissive reflects self-contained, disciplined happiness, as in *I'm better than what's around me and I'll see my way through on my own.*

Buoyancy: It's an ugly truth, but no less real all the same: some people simply enjoy feeling superior to others. Whether doing so boosts or merely affirms their self-esteem makes no difference. In a good, better, *I'm-the-best* scenario, a contempt verdict imposed on others leaves these people guilt-free to relish their success. Then the usual smirk combines with a higher level of happiness: maybe a big pleasure smile, or at least a satisfaction smile that lifts the cheeks (as shown here). Buoyancy is akin to *I'm having a good time savoring supremacy.* It's like pouring champagne for oneself while serving arsenic to everyone else.

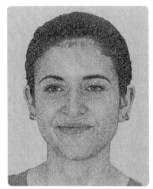

Buoyancy

Each Form's Top 10 List

How do contempt's four forms apply to the celebrities facially coded for this book? Across the board, musicians are overwhelmingly prominent. Only business people come anywhere close to being as frequently present, and that's mostly due to the presence of Bill Gates on every Top 10 list. Other celebrities who make more than one appearance consist of Elvis Presley, and two members of The Beatles: John Lennon and Ringo Starr. (Meanwhile, Khloe and Kim Kardashian each appear once.)

Scorched Earth: In general, an abrasive manner and a Scorched Earth expression are likely to go together. I'll give you a vivid example. In San Francisco to audition for his record contract with Warner Brothers, an 18-year-old Prince finds time to go see Carlos Santana. This is how Prince's first manager remembers the meeting:[15] "We open the door. It's an all-white house with all-white carpeting. Carlos says, 'Come in, please. Please take off your shoes.' I say, 'Prince, you gotta remove your boots.'

> ### TOP 10
> ## Scorched Earth
> Douglas MacArthur
> Eminem
> Joseph McCarthy
> Khloe Kardashian
> John Bonham
> Kanye West
> Bill Gates
> Leonardo DiCaprio
> Prince
> Jimi Hendrix

But Prince replies, 'I don't remove my boots for anyone.'" What's the outcome? The two musicians chat while the manager cleans up a trail of mud.

Prince aside, how about the other celebrities in the Top 10 list for Scorched Earth? Are any of them mild mannered? The answer is certainly *no* in regards to Led Zepplin's John Bonham, who died in his sleep at age 32 after consuming 40 shots of vodka. Such behavior wasn't unusual for a drummer whose highly energetic solos during the group's instrumental song "Moby Dick" often lasted for half an hour on stage. At times, Bonham would deliberately break his drumsticks part way through his solo and resort to banging on his drum kit with bloodied, bare hands.

Vindication: Early in his career, Hugh Hefner tended to express anger, contempt, and happiness. That's the Hefner who launched *Playboy* magazine in 1953. Back in those days, *no* out-weighed *yes*: anti-homosexual and anti-interracial marriage laws still ruled the land, and The Pill was not yet available. (Why, even using the word "pregnant" on TV was not allowed.) As a result, Hefner's crusade for *male* sexual freedom—separating sex from sin—became for him a matter of righteous indignation.[16]

The early version of Hefner didn't qualify him for the Top 10 Vindication list. It's only later in life, when anger got largely replaced by sadness, that Hefner fit the mold. Always one to objectify women, the guy was by then pathetically out of date. His Los Angeles Playboy mansion had been sold to the billionaire owner of Twinkies, with the proviso that Hefner got to live out his days on the premises, playing some tennis and watching old movies.

> **TOP 10**
> # Vindication
> **Hank Aaron**
> **Hillary Clinton**
> **Bill Gates**
> **Donald Trump**
> **Cam Newton**
> **Roger Clemens**
> **Andy Warhol**
> **Ringo Starr**
> **Elvis Presley**
> **Barack Obama**

Among the celebrities in the Top 10 list for Vindication, it could be said that Andy Warhol and Elvis Presley most clearly echoed Hefner's libertine lifestyle and decline. Another trio that also catches my attention on this list consists of Hank Aaron, Cam Newton, and Barack Obama. These African-Americans soon found in their careers a need to transcend prejudice related to the color of their skin. As an "ambassador" for his race, for example, Obama likes to quote Martin Luther King, Jr.'s statement that "The arc of the moral universe is long, but it bends toward justice." Needless to say, such a viewpoint requires great patience amid countless disappointments involving likely or suspected racism.

Dismissive: With the ultra-competitive Lindsey Vonn, it's all about grit and being "the captain of the ship."[17] She's shown plenty of take-charge contempt in becoming the most successful American ski racer ever. But a complicated life on and off the slopes may contribute to Vonn not consistently showing the mild happiness required for her to make the Top 10 Dismissive list. As a racer, the number of injuries Vonn has sustained during practices and competitions is astonishing. For instance, she's won races while skiing with her arm in a brace. Regarding her personal life, "I did my own thing for a while" is the way Vonn laconically describes a six-year lapse in talking to her dad after having been coached by him until the age of 16. While ambivalent about relationships with guys like ex-boyfriend Tiger Woods, for Vonn men remain the yardstick in measuring toughness: her favorite attribute. Vonn praises her grandfather as a role model and says of having raced downhill against men, "I definitely send some home crying."

TOP 10
Dismissive

Estee Lauder
Kim Kardashian
J. K. Rowling
Elvis Presley
Aretha Franklin
John Lennon
Amy Schumer
Jimmy Page
Bill Gates
Madonna

The Top 10 list for Dismissive is full of equally "feisty" women, to use Vonn's term for herself and others whose fighting spirit means they never surrender. I'll single out two of the women here. A natural affinity for feistiness links Aretha Franklin to Madonna, with Franklin perhaps most famous for her song "Respect". Meanwhile, Madonna's unabashedly strong, free-spirited stance is encapsulated in songs like "Express Yourself."

Buoyancy: Movie producer Arthur Freed said of Judy Garland, there's "not a mean bone in her body." Yes, it's true: anger was a rare emotion for the singer of "Somewhere Over the Rainbow" in *The Wizard of Oz* (1939). Garland nevertheless had

TOP 10
Buoyancy

John Lennon
Brian Jones
Ringo Starr
Tom Brady
Bill Gates
Ray Croc
Martha Stewart
Judy Garland
Paul McCartney
Mariah Carey

enough life experiences to soon come armed with contempt for the situations she faced. Pushy movie studio executives and disloyal spouses made life stressful. For example, one husband threatened to seek custody of Garland's children in a divorce if she didn't keep up her lucrative work load of live shows as well as TV and radio appearances.[18] In short, Garland always had her talent and appreciative fans, but caring husbands *not so much.*

Buoyancy is about extreme confidence and finding ways to enjoy yourself. In the Top 10 list for Buoyancy is Paul McCartney, who admitted that "At the end of The Beatles, I was really done in for the first time in my life. Until then, I really was a kind of cocky sod." When you see a smirk enlivened with a strong smile, you get the sense that these are people sure they've got it made. Selling lots of records (five singers are listed here), or software (Bill Gates), or hamburgers (Ray Croc) can do that for you.

Summary

Commonly defined as a mixture of disgust and anger, contempt is actually more a matter of *pressure* and *pleasure.* The accepted formula of anger plus disgust equals contempt supplies the pressure. The drive to achieve and set a higher standard of conduct for oneself is frequently a big part of why a person feels contempt. In regards to pleasure, bear in mind the happiness people may enjoy in concluding that, by comparison, they're better than the object of derision. Rather than *you're okay, I'm okay,* contempt is often more a matter of *you're mediocre (at best), which means I'm right to feel pretty good about myself.*

Is there a social virtue to feeling contempt? Yes, there is because contempt can serve as a non-verbal means of warning loved ones that so-and-so is a "bad apple." If valid, that judgment can help to protect a community by alerting its members to guard themselves against harmful, unfair people. Beyond that point, however, the virtues of contempt get cloudier. In evaluating others regarding who you think they truly are, defects and all, you're most likely also affirming yourself. While another person doesn't meet some implied standard, you do. So an ego boost of self-praise remains a big part of contempt. To display this emotion may, in effect, be a means of asserting one's greater power, status, ability, and integrity, too, relative to whomever or whatever is subject to dismissal.

Disgust

Turning Away

What Disgust Means

Billie Jean King enters the Astrodome's temporarily installed tennis court as Queen Cleopatra. Decorated with pink and white ostrich feathers, the litter holding her aloft is being carried by a team of four muscular men dressed as ancient slaves. It's September 20, 1973, and King's opponent for the evening's "Battle of the Sexes" tennis match is Bobby Riggs. He arrives in a rickshaw pulled by "Bobby's Bosom Buddies," all dressed in tight outfits. Riggs presents King with a giant candy sucker bearing the name of his corporate sponsor, Sugar Daddy. She in turn presents him with a piglet symbolizing male chauvinism.

The match with over 30,000 live spectators and a worldwide TV audience estimated at 90 million is pageantry as well as dead-serious business. Forget the $100,000, winner-take-all prize money. As the pre-match press conference confirms, there are much larger stakes involved.

A 55-year-old former Wimbledon champion, Riggs has recently beaten the world's number one ranked female player, Margaret Court, backing up his claim that the professional female tennis circuit is of inferior quality. For her part, King, age 29, and the ranking #2 female tennis player in the world, can't suppress a disgusted curl of her upper lip during the press conference. Looking over at Riggs, she vows to "put women's lib" where it belongs: in a place of honor. As King will later admit, "I thought it would set us back 50 years if I didn't win that match. It would ruin the women's [tennis] tour and affect all women's self-esteem."

Win King does, and she can laugh about subsequently appearing with Riggs in an episode of *The Odd Couple* entitled "The Pig Who Came to Dinner." For King and her fans, what doesn't change is that sexism remains morally intolerable and invites disgust: a feeling that something is either literally or figuratively akin to poison.

Like its "first cousin," contempt, disgust is a rejection-based, spurning emotion. Not a haughty feeling like contempt, disgust is in contrast a somewhat less dominant, more down-in-the-trenches emotion. Disgust isn't so much about *rising above* circumstances as it is about simply *getting away*. Consider the emotion's lowly, immediate, visceral origins. Something physically stinks or tastes bad. Universal triggers for disgust include:[1] feces, vomit, urine, mucus, and blood. In idiomatic terms, something *grosses us out*. For the vast majority of people, after a substance leaves our own body, we find it abhorrent—and that's doubly true of what belongs to another person.

Are there exceptions? Yes, blood-splattered horror films attract fans. In pursuit of pleasure, sex depends on overcoming any reservations we might have about physically comingling. But in general, people abhor on a basic, biological level the threat of contamination and take it seriously. Unlike the case with the emotions of anger and fear, on feeling disgust our heart rate *decreases*. We've stopped in our tracks to mull over something too "ugly" to approach more closely.

Outside of sensory threats, disgust likewise operates on a moral basis. We might find a person, idea, attitude, or specific behavior odious. What's unacceptable in those instances may qualify as offensive and repugnant, much like Riggs's chauvinism was for King in a match in which her vocation and entire gender were both under attack.

The slang term of being "fed-up" with something or someone fits this emotion well, linking the two basic modes of disgust: a momentary, visceral, sensory antipathy or a sustained, morally-infused revulsion. Further linking the two basic modes of disgust is the emotion's overall orientation. We're practicing avoidance. We have an aversive response and want to protect ourselves. Something akin to a gag reflex kicks in; feeling queasy or offended, we back off.

Given their often very tangible nature, the triggers for disgust can be very intimate. For example, a wrinkling nose may contract in order not to smell an offensive odor close at hand. Ultimately, though, disgust always leads to creating boundaries in order to keep our distance from whatever strikes us as objectionable. So in the end, (unless leavened by happiness) disgust becomes an intimacy-killing emotion likely to reduce our capacity for empathy and compassion.

Spotting Disgust

A disgusted face *recoils* as if the person has been confronted by a dead skunk. The physical essence of disgust is evasive action. More specifically, disgust appears in five ways on the face. Twice, disgust is the only emotion being shown on a person's face, as illustrated here:

Nose

The nose wrinkles and turns up, and the nostrils may flare.

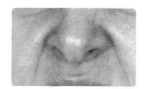

Mouth

The lower lip pulls down and, in stretching slightly wider, the lower lip may either flatten or stick out more.

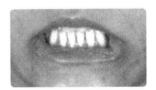

There are also another three cases in which disgust mingles with at least one extra emotion:

Cheeks & Mouth

The upper lip curls, the nostrils flare, and the skin pouches alongside the nose. The expression here shows a slightly unilateral, one-sided curl, which indicates some contempt.
(disgust, anger, contempt)

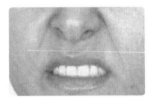

Mouth

The corners of the mouth sag.
(disgust, sadness)

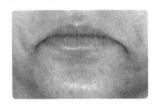

Mouth & Chin

The chin's dimpled skin rises and the mouth forms an upside-down smile.
(disgust, anger, sadness)

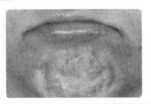

Disgust's Top 10 List

Among the celebrities analyzed for *Famous Faces Decoded*, disgust is almost as rare of an emotion as contempt. On average, just under 4% of the emoting involves disgust. But way back in the hunter-gatherer era, you can imagine how helpful and frequent the visceral, sensory mode of disgust could be. Our ancestors had to make gut-level decisions, like whether to bypass an overly-ripe fruit or a slimy watering hole. Wrong choices could leave them incapacitated and more vulnerable to predators.

Most Disgust

Roger Clemens
Barack Obama
Andy Warhol
Serena Williams
Greg Norman
Hank Aaron
John McEnroe
Aaron Rodgers
LeBron James
Elvis Presley

Least Disgust

Aretha Franklin
James Dean
Estee Lauder
Edward Snowden
Martha Stewart
Kim Kardashian
Edward R. Murrow
Walt Disney
Ray Croc
Martin Luther King*
Princess Diana*
*two-way tie

In terms of possible gender differences, the book's male celebrities reveal a small but proportionally far greater likelihood to show this feeling than their female counterparts. In the Top 10 list for Most Disgust, athletes abound. In my experience doing facial coding work in professional sports as well as for Division 1 NCAA teams, some of the greatest players are warriors whose feelings of disgust are driven by a strong, *internal* desire to constantly strive for success. Put another way, on an almost sensory basis they reject the status quo "stench" of mediocrity in favor of reaching another, higher level of physical performance.

In contrast, the disgust felt by Barack Obama, Andy Warhol, and Elvis Presley strikes me as more morally based and likely to reflect what they find unpleasant *around them*. In their cases, disgust might be more a matter of disengaging from what they find externally unwelcome, as in *this is dull or disagreeable, so I'm out of here.*

Among the Top 10 list for Least Disgust are celebrities less likely to dismiss possibilities or people out of hand. For instance, when asked about his sexual orientation, James Dean reportedly said: "No, I am not a homosexual. But I'm also not going to go through life with one hand tied behind my back." Likewise on this list is Martin Luther King Jr., who stayed *on-message* and *on-emotion* by continuing to advocate for nonviolent, civil disobedience despite the beatings his followers endured. It would have been *off-emotion* for him to give into disgust, thereby signaling rejection instead of the patience and enduring hope he exhibited.

How good are people at spotting disgust? Not so great, as it turns out. At 19%, disgust is in the cellar for detection accuracy, alongside fear. Indeed, if it weren't for Aaron Rodgers's example (covered in the previous chapter), voters would be collectively batting *zero* in terms of identifying this emotion as distinguishing the celebrities in the Top 10 Most Disgust list. That's because with Rodgers, at least, voters chose disgust as his second most above-average emotion by frequency, a judgment that matches the facial coding results.

As for the other nine celebrities on this list, disgust always gets ignored as a choice instead of the top billing it deserves. More specifically, the voting involves three different kinds of errors.

The first kind of error is that voters sometimes picked anger rather than disgust as more characteristic of these celebrities. Serena Williams, John

McEnroe, and Rogers Clemens belong in this group. Yes, it's hard to look past Clemens's bulldog, lips-tight expressions of anger in many photographs of him. But if you do, you'll also notice frequent signs of disgust: especially, a broadly curled upper lip and, at times, a wrinkled nose, a raised chin, or drooping mouth corners. What did Clemens reject as a baseball player? In amassing a record seven Cy Young pitching awards, he was so focused on winning that he responded to allegations of steroid abuse by saying, "I could care less about the rules."

Moving on from disgust misidentified as anger, another kind of error involves disgust-prone celebrities mistaken by voters as prone to sadness instead. Into this group put the golfer Greg Norman (known as The Shark); the artist Andy Warhol (nicknamed Drella by associates who saw his personality as being part Dracula, part Cinderella); and the "King of Rock 'n' Roll": Elvis Presley.

With Presley, a curled upper lip went along with rejecting the importance of money. "Elvis detested the business side of his career," Presley's first wife, Priscilla, observed, adding that Presley "would sign a contract without even reading it." Colonel Tom Parker, Presley's manager, liked that kind of behavior just fine, taking first a 25% commission and later on nearly 50% of Presley's earnings.[2]

Finally, the third kind of error involves celebrities mistakenly seen by voters as entirely happy in nature. Here, we're talking about two sports stars, Hank Aaron and LeBron James; plus one politician, Barack Obama, who rejects small-mindedness. In Obama case, his signature disgust expressions include both an upward chin thrust and his lower lip pulling down and away. Verbally, Obama's most revealing moment relevant to disgust was his remark that small-town voters "get bitter" and "cling to guns or religion or antipathy to people who aren't like them." That's a viewpoint his 2008 Democratic primary rival, Hillary Clinton, pounced on as "elitist" in nature.[3]

Barack Obama

Voted

happiness
happiness

Actual

disgust
contempt

Rare

satisfaction

What May Cause Disgust

The essence of disgust is rejection, as we seek to distance ourselves from whatever causes an aversive reaction. Unlike the more cerebral, attitudinal emotion of contempt, with disgust it's not that we distrust or disrespect someone or something per se. Instead, it's more a matter of a gut-level abhorrence of whatever triggered our response, as the following seven causes make evident.

1. What our senses take in strikes us as unhealthy; the input is unwelcome or potentially even harmful.

By game four of the 2016 NBA finals, the Golden State Warriors' spark plug, Draymond Green, and the Cleveland Cavaliers' superstar, LeBron James, have been mixing it up repeatedly. In this game, the two players get entangled, tumbling to the floor. As James steps over Green to rejoin the play, the sprawled Warrior seems to take a swipe at James's groin region. Nerves are raw. Among the players crowded together on court during the next stoppage of play, Green is making taunts that James responds to by showing his signature disgust expression: an upside down "smile" that may resemble a pout as James objects to Green's antics.

The NBA head office decides it's seen enough, and Green gets suspended from the next game in the series. In response, Green's teammate Klay Thompson says, "It's a man's league" and, in regards to James, "I guess his feelings got hurt."[4] Thompson is indirectly referring to James's complaint that something derogatory, something that *smells bad*, got said on court after the tangle-up. Warriors fans take the hint. They bring "Cry Baby" signs to the next game, including one that names James the NBA's Most Valuable Baby. Somebody else brings a giant baby bottle to the Warriors' arena. Immune to insults meant to poison his self-esteem, James takes the Most Valuable Player award after having enabled the Cavaliers to win the championship.

2. We're bored, as if what we're experiencing has no taste at all.

Aspiring "to be plastic," to live without emotion, Andy Warhol feels like he's mirroring his early 1960's experience. Authenticity, originality, skill, and beauty are all getting washed away by commercialism. Nothing is sacred, so why pretend that it is? Warhol often shows disgust in the way the corners of his mouth droop. The art dealer Leo Castelli isn't happy, either. Warhol won't sign his Pop Art works, insisting that anonymity reinforces the message that everything is being subject to mass reproduction. As soon as Castelli threatens to exclude Warhol from his gallery, however, the artist relents. The compromise proves to be a signature stamp.[5] That way, Castelli can approach big-money collectors while Warhol can stay true to his bored-with-everything outlook as he mourns the death of individuality.

3. Concerns about death and decay typically provoke feelings of disgust because what's unhygienic may infect us.

How to explain Whitney Houston's frightening and sad fall from grace? A good place to start is Houston getting booed by some members of the audience at the 1989 Soul Train Music Awards for being an "oreo" (black only on the outside). That same night she meets Bobby Brown.

It's as if Houston then decides to fight her (alleged) infection—being an "oreo"—by rejecting her positive image. Soon, the singer is telling *Rolling Stone*: "I am nobody's angel. I can get down and dirty. I can get raunchy."[6]

Proving her point, Houston becomes famous for being infamous by appearing in the reality TV series *Being Bobby Brown*, aired by Bravo in 2005. "Kiss my ass!" she snaps in one scene. The signature remark that signals Houston's refusal to "play nice" and get along with others, though, becomes "Hell to the no," a remark prominent in an episode devoted to Mother's Day. Houston renames the holiday "Hell Day," supporting her opinion by how her lower lip curls down and out in disgust. That same expression occurs again when Brown presents Houston with a bouquet of flowers. Everything, *even flowers* apparently stink if you're not enjoying your life, which is Houston's predicament.

The show gets widely panned for its many compromising situations, but bad reviews are trivial problems compared to Houston's debilitating drug habit. When the star dies of a heart attack, one of Houston's aides tells a waiting VH1 TV crew (with unintentional irony) that Houston "can't make it" to the interview because "she's dead,"[7] having just been found submerged in a bathtub upstairs in her suite at the Beverly Hilton.

4. Short of being "poisoned," we also don't want to appear weakened in any way. Our vitality is affirmed by being the opposite of a flaccid "loser".

Early in baseball's 2000 season, Rogers Clemens beans Mike Piazza with a pitch. The resulting concussion forces Piazza to miss the All-Star game. It's hardly a freak occurence. Known for the hard-throwing, intimidating style that inspired his nickname, "Rocket" Clemens will ultimately rank 9th all-time among MLB pitchers for hitting the bodies of batters.

Now it's the World Series and Piazza is at the plate, facing the Rocket again. As Piazza swings, a fragment of his broken bat flies toward Clemens on the pitcher's mound. Picking it up, the Rocket uses a wrist-whipping motion to throw the fragment in front of Piazza running to first base. As he does so, Clemens's face becomes contorted by a strong, upward-chin-thrust expression (signaling disgust, anger, and sadness). It's as if Clemens is offended by a foreign object, Piazza's splintered bat, trying to infiltrate the kingdom of his pitcher's mound. Afterwards, Clemens claims: "I was fired up and emotional and flung the bat toward the [hitters'] on-deck circle where the batboy was. I had no idea that Mike was running."[8]

Fined $50,000 for the "inappropriate" bat toss, Clemens will also, after his retirement, face scrutiny for his alleged steroids abuse. In defense, Clemens will ascribe his enduring prowess to a regimen of strenuous work-outs, not to mention odd rituals like having searingly hot muscle liniment applied to his private parts during post-game rub-downs. (Yes, it's yet another case of true stories often being stranger than fiction.)

5. We reject what feels morally tainted, looking to protect our values and integrity.

From the start, Serena Williams's father and initial, long-time tennis coach Richard Williams sets the agenda. He prepares Serena and her sister Venus for any and all racism ahead by paying for busloads of local kids to ring the practice courts in Compton, California, and shout the foulest things possible. Serena doesn't back down. Her signature expression is how her nose wrinkles in disgust, dismissing whatever she can't abide.

Taken to extremes, that stance can lead to a mishap like the time in 2009 when Serena threatens to stuff a tennis ball down a lineswoman's throat at the U.S. Open. Most times, however, Serena doesn't lose focus. She stands alone for having won a major tournament a record three times after facing match point during a two-week schedule of matches. About the only contest that Serena hasn't won is more corporate endorsements than her less-accomplished, blonde rival Maria Sharapova. If racial bias taints the awarding of those endorsement contracts, Serena doesn't say. Instead, she sticks to readily admitting that "I play for me" while also recognizing that, as a black female role model, she battles to represent "something much greater" than herself alone.[9]

6. Defending our boundaries, we cast off what we regard as strange and atypical.

America has never seen anything like it. Donald Trump comes down an escalator inside of Trump Tower to announce his candidacy for president on June 16, 2015, and promptly denounces foreigners. Besides ISIS, the countries of China, Japan, and Iran all get described as violating America's best interests. No country gets attacked more than Mexico, though, which is allegedly "sending people that have lots of problems, and they're bringing those problems" to America. So declares Trump with his most characteristic sign of disgust: an upward thrusting chin. "They're bringing drugs," the new candidate says, adding: "They're bringing crime. They're rapists. And some, I assume, are good people."

Trump's promise to "build a great, great wall on our southern border" is really an anti-promise, a vow to disavow others. In that way, it's no aberration. A germaphobe who prefers not to shake hands and who doesn't touch booze, drugs, or cigarettes, Trump is full of dislikes. For him disgust can apply to whole classes of people, enveloping racial and religious minorities as well as America's majority: women. Trump describes Rosie O'Donnell as a "big fat pig," while Megyn Kelly has "blood coming out of her wherever." Only family members are immune. For everyone else, there's Trump's signature phrase from *The Apprentice* (2004–2015)—"You're fired"—which constitutes yet another case of rejecting perceived impurities. Time and again, Trump's tweets read like bullying snorts of derision for others.

7. Fed-up and sick of it, we inoculate ourselves against a hostile social environment.

Sam Phillips, the owner of Sun Records in Memphis, has lately been saying: "If I could find a white man who had the Negro sound and the

Negro feel, I could make a billion dollars." Living in town is a poor, as-yet-unknown young man named Elvis Presley, who happens to know and appreciate black culture.[10] Before Presley's family moved to Memphis when the future star was 13 years old, the family had lived in Tupelo, Mississippi, where Presley would bring his guitar to gatherings in the nearby "colored" section of town.

In early July, 1954, a Memphis DJ plays a newly-covered song on the radio and soon the switchboard at WHBQ is lighting up. *Who's the artist? Who's singing "That's All Right, Mama"?* Quickly tracked down in a local movie theater, Presley find himself giving his first radio interview. *Where did you go to high school, son?* The DJ is asking as a way of letting white audiences know the singer is one of them, thanks to the whites-only, segregated school that is Presley's alma mater.[11]

Acceptance won't always come so easily. After Presley's first appearance in Las Vegas in 1956, a *Newsweek* critic will deride his act as akin to "a jug of corn liquor at a champagne party." Also put off, a judge in Jacksonville, Florida, will object to Elvis-the-Pelvis's stage antics, ordering Presley to tone things down. Besides dabbling in his usual upper lip curl, Presley's response to the judge will be to wiggle his little finger very suggestively while onstage the next time he performs in Florida.

Four Forms of Disgust

One of the most notable ways that disgust's theme of rejection gets expressed is when a MLB umpire calls a batter out on a third strike.[12] Many umpires use what's been called the *Invisible Chainsaw* motion, where the arm goes out, then pulls back, as if an umpire is ripping the cord of a chainsaw or lawn mower. Other umpires throw an *Uppercut*. And a few *Pick an Apple*, as if pulling down an unseen tree branch to get the fruit. That's tough competition in terms of memorable names, but here's my take on describing four forms of disgust.

DISGUST on a SPECTRUM

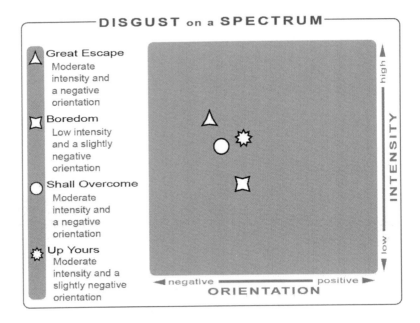

Great Escape
Moderate intensity and a negative orientation

Boredom
Low intensity and a slightly negative orientation

Shall Overcome
Moderate intensity and a negative orientation

Up Yours
Moderate intensity and a slightly negative orientation

INTENSITY — high / low

ORIENTATION — ◀ negative — positive ▶

Two of these forms involve disavowing, withdrawal reactions. People displaying the Great Escape or Boredom look want to avoid whatever is distasteful. Of those two, the Great Escape is more active and Boredom more passive. In contrast, the remaining forms combine disgust with the *hit-or-hug*, approach emotions of anger or happiness. Shall Overcome takes the anger route, while Up Yours combines disgust and mild happiness.

More specifically, each form of disgust gets shown as follows:

Great Escape: This look gets expressed in any or all of these ways: a wrinkling, upturned nose; a curling upper lip; or a lower lip pulling down and slightly outward, as if somebody is sucking on a really bitter lemon. It's the wrinkled nose and raised lip that are abundantly on display in the

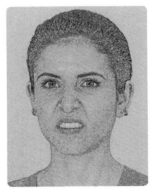

Great Escape

photo before you. People who exhibit such strong signals of disgust want to escape feeling contaminated. The person, object, situation, or place that triggers these kinds of reactions can't be left behind quickly enough.

Boredom: In this era of entertainment, we expect to be endlessly enthralled and amused. So something dull with no taste to it is, for lots of people, likely to be even worse than something in bad taste. Indifference kills TV ratings and many a conversation. Feeling let down and bored may lead to a frown alone, or be combined with the mouth falling ever so slightly open, as if the person

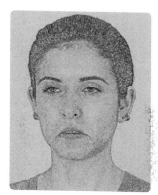

Boredom

is suppressing a yawn. Eyes dimmed and lowered, as evident in this case, is another possible signal to add to the ways that sadness appears.

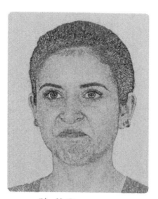

Shall Overcome

Shall Overcome: Witness the convergence of two *don't-tread-on-me* emotions: namely, disgust and anger. An upraised chin that puckers, tightened lips, and either a wrinkled nose or a raised upper lip—as shown here—becomes the expressive package. It signals a determination not to accept what is, and instead resist and overcome challenges to one's preferred outcome.

Up Yours: At times, a wrinkled nose or a raised upper lip merges with a slight smile. (The accompanying photo shows the raised upper lip option; the strong cheek pouches either side of the nose are the dead

Up Yours

give-away.) *How strange*, you might say. *How can disgust and happiness cohabitate?* And yet it's a pretty common look. In rebellion against the status quo, some people readily blend these two emotions. Why not, when they find it satisfying to take sweet revenge on whatever they find disagreeable by turning the situation to their advantage.

Each Form's Top 10 List

How do disgust's four forms apply to the celebrities facially coded for this book? One observation is that Hollywood actors are fairly common here. But for two other professions, differences emerge. With the more evasive, disengaged forms of Great Escape and Boredom, athletes abound. In contrast, the musicians who appear in these Top 10 lists favor the defiant forms of Shall Overcome and Up Yours. Overall, the recurring celebrities consist of Jane Fonda, Elvis Presley, Hank Aaron, and Khloe Kardashian, with plenty of women representing Hollywood as well as the music industry.

Great Escape: What does Kate Winslet want to escape from? Quite a lot, as it turns out. Topics she doesn't much want to discuss with the press include: Hollywood's gender bias, which means bigger contracts for its male stars (too "vulgar" to address "out in the open"); and the actress's weight ("once a fat kid, always a fat

TOP 10

Great Escape

Hank Aaron
Roger Clemens
Jimi Hendrix
Kate Winslet
Khloe Kardashian
Elvis Presley
Will Smith
Serena Williams
Ringo Starr
Jack Nicklaus

kid").[13] Winslet might have played a socialite traveling first class in *Titanic* (1997), but "I didn't come from the fancy home, no," she freely admits in interviews laced with obscenities.

Who else is in the Top 10 list for the Great Escape? Prominent is Jimi Hendrix, who told a *Rolling Stone* reporter a year before his death: "I don't want to be a clown anymore. I don't want to be a rock and roll star."[14] Hendrix is joined by three other African-Americans. (The total climbs to fully half this list if we include Khloe Kardashian, who was fathered by O. J. Simpson,[15] at least according to Simpson's friend and former manager Norman Pardo.) Topping the list of those turned off by what they've encountered is Hank Aaron. That persevering slugger never forgot the time in his Negro League days when he heard the white restaurant staff breaking all the plates on which the team's players had just finished eating.

Boredom: For a guy with skin described as "perpetually the color of mayonnaise," Larry Bird sure hated to have another white guy guard him. To Bird, that wasn't enough of a challenge. Consider the time the basketball star turned to Chicago Bulls coach Doug Collins, sitting courtside, and guffawed, "Are you fucking kidding me?" about the Caucasian no-name player trying to hold down his point total. On another occasion, a bored Bird decided to shoot left-handed for a game and had 27 points after three quarters.

TOP 10

Boredom

Andy Warhol
Larry Bird
Adele
Jackie Robinson
Beyonce
Ted Williams
John McEnroe
Marilyn Monroe
Diane Keaton
Jane Fonda

Bird's on-court antics prove he was no slouch when it came to fighting against the Boredom he felt. Another Boston sports legend, Ted

Williams, also appears in the Top 10 list for Boredom. That baseball star's loathing for whatever disinterested him was so colorful a reporter called him "Our Hemingway. He writes our stories for us." Then there's John McEnroe, whose decision to stop playing tennis doubles with Peter Fleming was fatal to his career because of McEnroe's intolerance for doing drills. Mens' doubles matches had often been McEnroe's only real "practice" sessions for his more important singles matches, and now those warm-ups had gone away.

Shall Overcome: While Kanye West began his career as a producer using pitched-up vocal samples to enact a musical style sometimes mocked as "chipmunk soul," you wouldn't know it now. West has appeared on the cover of *Rolling Stone* wearing a crown of thorns (appropriately enough for a guy who proclaims: "I'm like a vessel, and God has chosen me to be the voice and the connector"). If Jesus comparisons aren't enough, try Michael Jackson, Leonardo da Vinci, and Steve Jobs among the litany of greats West puts himself in league with. Then in 2016, West literally upped the ante. In a Twitter posting, the musician told Mark Zuckerberg he should "invest 1 billion dollars" in West's ideas to support the "greatest artist of all time."[16]

TOP 10

Shall Overcome
Aaron Rodgers
Douglas MacArthur
Barry Bonds
Barack Obama
J. K. Rowling
Prince
Eminem
Kanye West
Elton John
George Wallace

The Top 10 list for Shall Overcome includes some of the strongest personalities found in *Famous Faces Decoded*. There's Aaron Rogers ("I think very highly of myself"); Barry Bonds ("I like to be against the odds. I'm not afraid to be lonely at the top"); and Elton John ("There is nothing wrong with going to bed with someone of your own sex. People should be very free with sex, [though] they should draw the line at goats.") Clearly, people who combine disgust with anger have no problem being brazen.

Up Yours: Through her stage costumes, lyrics, and the imagery in her musical videos, Madonna has always pushed boundaries. This musical artist insists on autonomy. "Papa Don't Preach" is but one illustrative song title. As to imagery, her "Like a Prayer" video showcases the erotic dream of making love to a saint, a move that brought Madonna both condemnation and publicity. When you're the best-selling female recording artist ever and second behind The Beatles on *Billboard's* Greatest of All Time list, then you've earned the right to entitle your greatest-hits album *The Immaculate Collection* (1990).

While Madonna's fluid, ever-evolving image has, at times, echoed in style Marilyn Monroe's persona, another, different sex symbol in the Top 10 list for Up Yours is Elizabeth Taylor. Many of the celebrities on this list have bigger-than-life personalities, and Taylor is certainly a case in point. During the transition from childhood star to ingenue, Taylor was asked: "Elizabeth, where on earth did you ever learn how to make love like that?" The question came from Hollywood gossip columnist Hedda Hopper after she saw Taylor's performance in *A Place in the Sun* (1951).[17] Taylor was bold, concluding that people with "no vices" generally "have some pretty annoying virtues." Fast forward to Taylor leaving her fourth husband, Eddie Fisher, for Richard Burton. There again was Taylor going her own way, exhibiting behavior the Vatican would publicly condemn as constituting "erotic vagrancy."

TOP 10

Up Yours

Amy Schumer
Elvis Presley
Jimmy Page
Aretha Franklin
Madonna
Jane Fonda
Khloe Kardashian
Steven Spielberg
Elizabeth Taylor
Hank Aaron

Summary

What innately triggers disgust includes, but isn't limited to, anything physically inopportune, strange to us, or morally tainted. Something "stinks" or, alternatively, is so boring it seemingly has no taste or smell at all. Put off, we back off. Given its often sensory nature, disgust can originate as a very intimate emotion, but it always leads to creating boundaries. We like to keep our distance from whatever strikes us as repellant. Therefore, disgust typically reduces our capacity for empathy and compassion.

We reject what we consider bad, encompassing anyone or anything that lands on a scale somewhere between "yucky" to "poisonous". People experience disgust on a sensory level early in life (kids tend to be finicky eaters). Then the morally based version of disgust becomes a greater factor as our beliefs and values take firm, even permanent shape, a move that most often happens as we go from being teenagers to adults. While the related emotion of contempt comes more from the head, disgust is a gut-level verdict rejecting anything that doesn't meet our tastes.

*f*lash

Personality insights revealed by
facial coding comparisons

{ parallel

careers }

Oprah Winfrey		
Voted	**Actual**	**Rare**
happiness	*joy*	contempt
happiness	*pleasure*	

Ellen DeGeneres		
Voted	**Actual**	**Rare**
happiness	*joy*	sadness
happiness	*pleasure*	

Hugely successful talk show hosts who both hail from the Deep South, Ellen DeGeneres and Oprah Winfrey also have in common upbringings that involved sexual molestation.[1] How have they come through their respective experiences? Emotionally, the answer is on identical terms— just as voters predicted. These two women are amazingly upbeat. Any difference between them centers instead on which emotion each feels *least* often. For the effervescent DeGeneres, who doubles as a stand-up comedian, it's sadness. In Winfrey's case, she hardly registers any contempt for others after having grown up so poor that her dresses were humbly made of potato sacks.

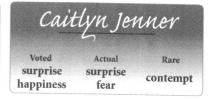

Bruce Jenner		
Voted	**Actual**	**Rare**
surprise	satisfaction	disgust
happiness	*pleasure*	

Caitlyn Jenner		
Voted	**Actual**	**Rare**
surprise	surprise	contempt
happiness	fear	

When Caitlyn Jenner was still Bruce Jenner, the 1976 Olympic decathlon winner, he felt like he was "always telling lies" as he gave promotional speeches while wearing panty hose and a bra under his suit.[2] In a long career as primarily a television personality, has the new identity made Jenner more content? The answer may be *no*. As Bruce, happiness was the more dominant emotional note. For Caitlyn, surprise and fear have been the most prevalent. That change is in keeping with her confession: "the uncomfortableness of being me never leaves all day long." The good news is that free of playing Bruce, the masculine, all-American hero, Caitlyn feels less contempt. She's no longer living a life that feels deceitful.

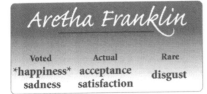

Aretha Franklin		
Voted	Actual	Rare
happiness	acceptance	disgust
sadness	satisfaction	

Diana Ross		
Voted	Actual	Rare
happiness	*pleasure*	sadness
happiness	acceptance	

Voters saw happiness in both of these singers, but less so in Aretha Franklin. And in that, they were correct. The Queen of Soul's version of happiness isn't as upbeat as is true of former Supremes' lead singer Diana Ross. What's most interesting here, however, is which emotion each singer rarely shows. It's sadness for Ross, who has never publicly regretted monopolizing the microphone when the Supremes attempted the group's first reunion. For Franklin, it's disgust. There is little she has the self-discipline to avoid indulging in, though she's learned "I wouldn't starve if I had one hot dog instead of two."[3]

Steve Jobs		
Voted	Actual	Rare
surprise	anger	sadness
sadness	surprise	

Bill Gates		
Voted	Actual	Rare
happiness	contempt	fear
happiness	satisfaction	

The two men were at first uneasy business allies, then bitter rivals on the way to ultimately becoming friends of a sort.[4] Besides different commercial instincts, Bill Gates and Steve Jobs also had to navigate their different styles. Most of the harder, verbal jabs exchanged between them came from Jobs. "Gates has no shame" is but one example of Jobs's anger outwardly directed. Surprise was also true of Jobs, an often times wide-eyed innovator. But the sadness voters purported to see in Jobs was actually a rare emotion for him. By comparison, Gates runs cooler than Jobs. His version of a rebuke was to call Jobs "fundamentally odd," a put-down that conveys a sense of superiority based on feeling contempt and an utter lack of fear.

Jimi Hendrix				Prince		
Voted	**Actual**	**Rare**		**Voted**	**Actual**	**Rare**
surprise	anger	*pleasure*		happiness	contempt	fear
sadness	contempt			surprise	anger	

The pair of emotions that most distinguish these two legendary guitarists is interchangeably the same: anger and contempt (thereby throwing voters' choices out the window). Where the two men varied involves which emotion arose least often. For Prince, it was a lack of fear. Never one to pander, Prince turned the pinnacle of his commercial success into the moment he deconstructed the sound that got him there. In Jimi Hendrix's case, the answer is that he rarely felt pleasure. As if imprisoned by stardom, Hendrix began to quietly rebel by mumbling "etcetera etcetera" in interviews. The girlfriend he lived with remembers seeing Hendrix smile only when he was jamming and "got it right for himself, not for anyone else."[5]

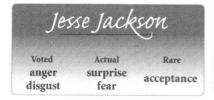

Jesse Jackson				Martin Luther King		
Voted	**Actual**	**Rare**		**Voted**	**Actual**	**Rare**
anger	surprise	acceptance		anger	fear	disgust
disgust	fear			happiness	surprise	

People often "see" what they expect to see, and here's a striking example. Voters saw both of these civil rights icons as predominantly *angry*. In truth, the two emotions that distinguish Jesse Jackson and Martin Luther King Jr. are surprise and fear. Does King have more of a halo around his image? Perhaps, as voters also ascribed to him the more upbeat emotion of mild happiness. For Jackson, the voters thought disgust accompanied anger. Rarely given to slight smiles, Jackson has nevertheless delivered this example of sly humor: "Poor people lie, rich people prevaricate."

Rush Limbaugh		
Voted	**Actual**	**Rare**
anger	anger	fear
contempt	disgust	

Howard Stern		
Voted	**Actual**	**Rare**
contempt	satisfaction	sadness
anger	anger	

Voters didn't perceive these two radio "shock jocks" as being very different, emotionally speaking, and they're correct in that anger defines both Rush Limbaugh and Howard Stern to a large degree. A big emotional difference that does exist between them, however, is hinted at by the titles of books they published a year apart: *The Way Things Ought to Be* (1992) by Limbaugh, and *Private Parts* (1993) by Stern. In the end, what does satisfaction-oriented Stern want? To have fun, sex, money, and great ratings is surely the answer. For Limbaugh, a focus on politics leads to what supporters view as fearless, courageous, red-meat attacks on liberals. Trying to shape America's body politic is what drives Limbaugh to challenge what he finds repugnant.

Mick Jagger		
Voted	**Actual**	**Rare**
happiness	*joy*	*pleasure*
happiness	surprise	

Keith Richards		
Voted	**Actual**	**Rare**
happiness	acceptance	sadness
anger	disgust	

A journalist who has long covered The Rolling Stones[6] says of Mick Jagger, he's "Elvis in a gold lamé jacket." In comparison, Keith Richards is "the friend who won't let you forget the promise you made under the bridge." Voters saw Jagger as happy and rightly so, given the lead singer's flashy expressions of joy and surprise. Richards is different. The guy who tagged Jagger's 2001 solo album *Goddess in the Doorway* as "Dogshit in the Doorway" after their friendship collapsed, instead favors acceptance (the lowest, most begrudging version of happiness), along with disgust.

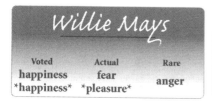

Willie Mays		
Voted	Actual	Rare
happiness	fear	
happiness	*pleasure*	anger

Hank Aaron		
Voted	Actual	Rare
happiness	disgust	
happiness	contempt	acceptance

These two great African-American baseball stars grew up in Alabama, but there the similarity ends. "Mays is city, Aaron country," one sportswriter noted,[7] citing the time that Willie Mays sat in on one of Hank Aaron's TV interviews and razzed him with comments like "Hank! You just fall off the turnip truck?" Yes, happiness was a prominent part of Mays and his "Say Hey Kid" personality. Absent from voters' take on Mays, however, was the degree to which fear shadowed him. Meanwhile, voters got Aaron *all* wrong. They missed how the spurning emotions of disgust and contempt helped Aaron respond in kind to baseball fans who disliked having a black player overtake Babe Ruth's home run record.

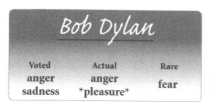

Bob Dylan		
Voted	Actual	Rare
anger	anger	
sadness	*pleasure*	fear

Bruce Springsteen		
Voted	Actual	Rare
happiness	*pleasure*	
anger	acceptance	surprise

There have been lots of singer-songwriters heralded as "the next Bob Dylan."[8] By now a long-standing star in his own right, Bruce Springsteen was at first given that moniker because of his rough-hewn voice and compelling lyrics. Granted, both men have never seen eye-to-eye with authority figures, including their fathers. They're nevertheless not emotionally very similar. A scowling, angry Dylan has, as voters saw, largely eclipsed the earlier version of Dylan: a singer who sometimes laughed aloud while recording a song. In contrast, anger isn't an emotion that describes Springsteen. Instead, his pleasure in being on stage enthralling a live audience remains as true today as it was back in the era when *Born to Run* (1975) catapulted Springsteen and his E Street Band to fame.

part **3** three

reactive

emotions

Surprise

Change Is Afoot

What Surprise Means

For a few hours on November 10, 2014, Bill Cosby's public relations team posts on billcosby.com a meme generator: a free online image maker. The entry comes complete with a photograph of a grinning Cosby and the statement, "Hello my name is Bill Cosby, I am the star of the classic 90s comedy 'Ghost Dad.' Also I am a serial rapist."[1] A tweet from Cosby's account simultaneously invites response by urging, "Go ahead. Meme me!" What kind of captions Cosby expects people to add to his photo, who knows? This pair of strange postings does nothing to slow down the fast-moving transformation of Cosby's public image from beloved, cuddly funnyman to sexual predator.

To reconstruct how Cosby's image gets altered, I need to start in early 2014 with a different case, involving another celebrity, to pinpoint what indirectly initiates the change. That's when Dylan Farrow publishes a letter in *The New York Times*, reminding readers in very personal terms of accusations that Woody Allen had raped her during her childhood over two decades ago. *What other icons might have skeletons in the closet?* Three days later, *Gawker* publishes a story about the multiple sexual assault accusations levelled against Cosby for his behavior a decade ago.

Before long, numerous women are presenting their own, additional allegations regarding Cosby and a time period stretching from the mid-1960s to 2008. Then the comedian Hannibal Buress develops a stand-up act that features remarks calling Cosby a "rapist". After a video of the act goes viral, Buress gets interviewed by Howard Stern. Explaining his motivation for launching the anti-Cosby routine, Buress suggests Cosby's hypocrisy for telling young black people how to live: "Yeah, but you raped women, Bill Cosby. So, brings you down a couple notches."

Following the Stern interview, Cosby's public relations team posts the meme-generator stunt. Now things really heat up. Cosby cancels an interview on the *Late Show with David Letterman*; NBC cancels its plan for a new comedy in which Cosby will play a wise grandfather; and on NPR, Cosby says literally not a single word to refute the new felony charges, despite being given numerous opportunities to do so. *How perplexing.* Thereby proven powerful again is surprise, an emotion about the various mysteries in life that make us pay attention.

Among the seven core emotions, surprise belongs in a category by itself for two reasons. The first is its *brevity.* While the other emotions may last a few seconds, then resurface repeatedly over time based on a specific triggering detail being recalled, surprise functions like a pre-emotion. Surprise happens quickly—in a second or less, if genuinely felt. Then it's done and gone because a real surprise can't be a surprise twice over.

The second unique quality concerns surprise's *supposed neutrality.* This emotion is typically classified as neither positive nor negative (unlike the other six emotions in this book, which get stereotyped erroneously as simply being either positive or negative in nature, when in fact they can have both good and bad implications). Surprise alone is thought of as merely setting the stage for other emotions to weigh in. Now let me complicate that assumption of neutrality with dual examples of when a surprise might happen. Maybe your parents give you *a new car* for the holidays. Or maybe a stranger makes you part of *a new car accident* on your way home from work one day. You've just experienced a good or bad surprise.

During the first nano-seconds of a surprise, yes, your reaction might be essentially *neutral*. An emotional verdict awaits. And on occasion, after reflection, you realize that what's happened qualifies as ambiguous and, therefore, a *neutral*, mixed experience. Maybe for instance the gift of a new car comes with expectations that you'll improve your grades in college.

On balance, though, surprise encompasses two opposing instincts: *positive* curiosity and *negative* wariness. Curiosity reflects our natural desire to uncover knowledge. The pleasure of discovery activates parts of the brain that welcome rewards. In contrast, wariness arises when we're confronted by what's puzzling or conflicts with what we thought we knew. The resulting unpleasant feeling may involve cognitive dissonance and, instead, activates parts of the brain associated with suffering.[2]

Either way, in keeping with the Nature and Frequency of Emotions chart that appears in the introduction to *Famous Faces Decoded*, surprise joins fear in being a reactive emotion. That's because, for starters, surprise is a submissive as opposed to a dominant emotion. Again, the essence of surprise is that in a flash we face the unknown. Does pleasure or pain, or a combination thereof, await us? We don't know, and the mystery has power over us rather than the other way around.

At times, people clearly welcome surprises. Good movies and novels, like anything creative, depend on an element of surprise to keep us engaged. But in daily life, most people rarely welcome surprises because of the effort required to deal with them. Left to our own devices, lots of us welcome the opportunity to lounge around like house cats, only occasionally exerting ourselves. As a result, surprise has to be classified as an avoidance rather than as an approach emotion.

To reinforce that point, consider this basic truth about human nature. Behavioral economists research the role of emotion in people's decision-making process. Their studies find that we hear bad news *twice* as loudly as good news.[3] Our survival mechanisms prompt us to be more alert and prone to letting setbacks gnaw on us, rather than relish success. So it shouldn't be a shock that surprise and fear often go hand-in-hand in the way the two emotions get expressed, as you're about to learn.

Spotting Surprise

A surprised face *elongates* as if the face's reaction to a sudden, unexpected event is getting painted on a larger canvas than normal. More specifically, surprise never appears entirely on its own. There are instead four basic ways in which it emerges in conjunction with other core emotions:

Eyebrows

The inner part of one or both eyebrows lifts upwards, often creating forehead wrinkles.
(surprise, fear, sadness)

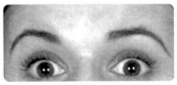

Eyebrows

The outer part of one or both eyebrows lifts upwards, often creating forehead wrinkles.
(surprise, fear)

Eyes

The eyes go wide as the upper eyelids rise.
(surprise, anger, fear)

Mouth & Jaw

The lips part and the jaw drops. Two degrees of response are shown here, moving from angular lip corners (upper photo) to an active stretching of the mouth that includes rounded corners and also the flattening and stretching of the cheeks and chin (lower photo). Whenever the mouth gets wider but remains more relaxed, rather than stretching tightly, then this facial display interpretively favors surprise over fear. *(surprise, fear)*

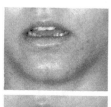
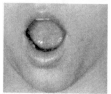

Finally, one extra point needs to be made here regarding surprise. Sometimes being *startled* is thought of as being *surprised*, but the two responses are different. With a startle, the eyes close, the brow lowers, and the mouth tenses. A startle reaction is a physical reaction, not a feeling. You can be startled without being surprised. For example, you want to set off some firecrackers on July 4th. It's therefore hardly unexpected when a loud boom jolts you.

Surprise's Top 10 List

Among the celebrities facially coded for *Famous Faces Decoded*, on average just over 8% of their feelings involve surprise. The results also show that male celebrities have a slightly higher average than their female counterparts, and that men dominate the Top 10 list for Most Surprise.

Again, since people rarely welcome surprises, it's no wonder that sur-

TOP 10

Most Surprise

Marilyn Monroe
Edward R. Murrow
Bill Cosby
Wayne Gretzky
Jimmy Stewart
Ingrid Bergman
Alfred Hitchcock
Jesse Jackson
Frank Sinatra
Little Richard

prise and fear have plenty of overlapping facial muscle movements. Marilyn Monroe, Bill Cosby, Wayne Gretzky, and Jimmy Stewart also appear in the following chapter's Top 10 list for Most Fear. Of those four celebrities, only Monroe shows more surprise than fear—a finding that refutes anybody who assumes that Monroe's anxiety crippled her natural inquisitiveness.

As for the other six celebrities in this list, they all show more surprise than fear—an outcome that suggests that for them positive curiosity outweighs negative wariness. Of those six, the intrepid journalist Edward R. Murrow most favors surprise, followed in descending order, from more to ever less of a mix in favor of surprise over fear, by Ingrid Bergman, Alfred Hitchcock, Little Richard, and Jesse Jackson. Then there's Frank Sinatra, the wariest of the lot, who only just barely shows more surprise than fear.

As to the celebrities in the Top 10 list for Least Surprise, again men predominate. What makes these men different from the men most given to surprise? It's probably fair to say that many of them qualify as too self-possessed or insular to be deeply interested in what others think or feel about them. Fitting that description could be, among others, the Rolling Stones' founder Brian Jones, and radio host Rush Limbaugh.

How good are people at spotting surprise? At 38%, this feeling comes in fifth among the eight emotional categories in terms of detection accuracy, behind sadness, but far ahead of sixth-place contempt. Two celebrities who voters did a good job emotionally diagnosing are men who practically made surprise their *raison*

TOP 10

Least Surprise

Douglas MacArthur
Brian Jones
Khloe Kardashian
David Letterman
John Bonham
Joseph McCarthy
Leonardo DiCaprio
Bill Wyman
Charles Schulz
Rush Limbaugh

d'etre. One of them is Alfred Hitchcock, "The Master of Suspense." The other is Little Richard, whose many nicknames are surprising in themselves: The Queen of Rock 'n' Roll, The Emancipator, and The Bronze Liberace being among them.

Bill Cosby

Voted

sadness anger

Actual

surprise fear

Rare

acceptance

Those two examples aside, the other eight celebrities in the Top 10 Most Surprise list aren't assessed correctly by voters. Into one camp fall celebrities seen as predominantly either sad or angry. There you'll find Marilyn Monroe, Jesse Jackson, and Bill Cosby, whose most notable way of expressing surprise is when his outer eyebrows rise. In happier times for him, Cosby was certainly capable of pleasant surprises himself. Who else would earn a Doctor of Education degree in the 1970s after having already starred in the TV show *I Spy*? (There was also by then Cosby's *To Russell, My Brother, Whom I Slept With* (1968), which *Spin* magazine has named the number one comedy album of all-time.)

With the other camp of celebrities misjudged by voters, the common thread is that they were seen as being downright happy. Not true, especially in Frank Sinatra's case given how often "Old Blue Eyes" eyes would go wide and his mouth fall slightly open, as if transfixed by the unexpected. That surprise is so flexible in orientation, from positive curiosity to negative wariness, suits perfectly Guy Talese's *Esquire* profile of Sinatra.[4] There, Talese writes: "The most distinguishing thing about Sinatra's face

Frank Sinatra

Voted

happiness *happiness*

Actual

surprise fear

Rare

anger

are his eyes, clear blue and alert, eyes that within seconds can go cold with anger, or glow with affection."

What May Cause Surprise

Surprise arises from a disruption of the status quo. Whether a surprise heralds pleasure, pain, or a blend of those two outcomes, change is afoot. Unlike the case with the other core emotions in this book, here only the first four causes address surprise's sudden nature. The final three "causes" are really about making adjustments. They focus on how people handle *learning moments*, which require them to acclimate to surprises and accordingly make changes in their lives.

1. Overconfidence leads to our over-estimating the likelihood of positive outcomes. So when reality intervenes, high hopes and expectations get dashed.

A reaction of "Oh, man, I am going to die" follows on first hearing the news from The Los Angeles Lakers' team doctor.[5] Now Earvin "Magic" Johnson is largely composed as he begins his November 7, 1991 retirement press conference by declaring, "Because of the HIV virus I have obtained, I will have to retire from the Lakers today." With that opening statement, Johnson's left eyebrow rises in a look of surprise and fear. Clearly, the point guard never expected to find himself in this situation. For anyone who's a star athlete, it must be tempting to imagine you're invincible and, therefore, immune to diseases, too, regardless of how you handle your private life.

Johnson's wife Cookie is newly pregnant with their son. Will the baby be safe? Did his wife contract the disease? For how long might Johnson live? It will be another five years before the invention of a life-saving, "triple cocktail" drug therapy means an HIV infection isn't a death sentence. Much about the disease remains unknown in 1991.

As Johnson discloses his plan to "become a spokesman for the HIV virus because I want people, young people, to realize that they can practice safe sex," his eyes go wide. Still trying to reconcile himself to this HIV bombshell announcement, Johnson will try returning to the NBA next year. But plagued by weakened knees and opposition from several players who feel he poses a health hazard, he will then retire for good.

2. In behavioral economics, the principle is known as "probability blinders." In other words, some surprises wouldn't be surprises at all if only we weren't so willfully blind regarding the likely consequences of our actions.

It's July of 1972, a little over a year before U.S. troops leave Vietnam and less than three years before the war finally ends. Jane Fonda's second husband, the anti-war activist Tom Hayden, has convinced her to visit Hanoi. There and in the surrounding landscape, Fonda sees firsthand the damage American bombing has done to the country. Easily the most indelible photographs from her visit are those of the actress beside an enemy anti-aircraft gun meant to shoot down U.S. planes. The photos often show Fonda with not only a wide-eyed look, but also a cocked right outer eyebrow and her mouth hanging ajar, as if bewildered by what's going on. An intense backlash follows her return to America.

In a 2011 entry on her official website, Fonda explains that a translator said some soldiers wanted to serenade her. "I hardly even thought about where I was sitting. The cameras flashed," Fonda writes. "It is possible that it was a set-up, that the Vietnamese had it all planned. I will never know." Then in post-surprise, retrospective mode, Fonda apologizes: "If I was used, I allowed it to happen ... a two-minute lapse of sanity that will haunt me forever." A reviewer of Fonda's autobiography, *My Life So Far*, ends up calling the actress "breathtakingly naive."[6]

3. Sometimes reality exceeds our expectations, leaving us feeling lucky and perhaps even downright incredulous.

Could her time on stage represent both the most extraordinarily earnest and shortest Academy Awards acceptance speech ever given? I'm talking about Audrey Hepburn winning Best Actress in 1954 for *Roman Holiday*. Here's the entire 32-second speech, which follows a stunned Hepburn reaching the stage, eyes down, at first accidentally turning away from the podium. "It's just too much," Hepburn falteringly begins, before gushing: "I want to say *thank you* to everybody who in these past months and years has helped, guided, and given me so much." A pause lets Hepburn catch her emotional breath. "I'm truly, truly grateful," the actress all but concludes. Then, as her demeanor of raised eyebrows but a downcast head gives way (at last) to a beaming, joyful smile, Hepburn adds, "and *terribly happy*." With that final verbal burst, the speech ends in hearty applause. It's affirmation once unimaginable for a woman whose frail frame is a vestige of her having nearly starved to death in her native Holland during World War Two.[7]

4. In treasuring the unexpected, our spontaneity can give rise to the unexpected naturally happening.

Who among us ever gets asked to stop singing in church? Little Richard does, for "screaming and hollering" so loudly his childhood nickname becomes "War Hawk." The boy who beats on house steps or pots and pans while singing eventually becomes the man famous for lifting one leg while playing piano, or jumping around atop the piano itself! As Little Richard ecstatically pumps his legs, often his eyebrows are shooting skyward and his mouth falls wide open, seemingly in astonishment at his own antics.

The first rock musician to use spotlights and flicker lights, the bi-sexual Little Richard takes the stage by storm, wearing makeup, colorful capes, blouses, and precious-stone-and-sequin-studded suits. The essence of experiencing Little Richard's act, however, remains hearing him *sing* in a raspy shout—*crooning*—*wailing*—*screaming*. What does it take to cover a song like "Tutti Frutti" (1956)? Paul McCartney recalls: "I could do Little Richard's voice, which is … like an out-of-body experience. You have to leave your current sensibilities and go about a foot above your head to sing it."

5. There are situations whereby a surprise mixes good and bad elements, and it will take time for us to understand the balance.

For the half-time show at the 2004 Super Bowl, Janet Jackson and Justin Timberlake are performing together. They're singing "Rock Your Body" and making all sorts of brief, suggestive body contact during the duet. Two lines from the lyrics stand out. First, Timberlake sings: "No disrespect, I don't mean no harm." Then he pulls off the rubber bustier covering Jackson's right breast as he croons, "Gotta have you naked by the end of this song." Viewers find themselves witnessing the *boob seen around the world*, until the CBS cameras retreat to a wide-angle shot of the stage.

What's Jackson's reaction? Just before the apparent mishap, her eyes were closed. But now as her whipping hair hides her face, she looks down over her chest. Next, she cups a hand across her exposed breast and gives Timberlake a wide-eyed, hard look. Jackson's glaring suggests she *is* in fact surprised by what's ocurred. For his part, Timberlake is still clutching the bustier as he momentarily closes his eyes and his eyebrows knit together, indicating dismay and concern with how the stunt has turned out.

Afterwards, attention turns to a pre-event story. The MTV website was promising "shocking moments" during Jackson's performance at the Super Bowl. Jackson's publicist insists the stunt was meant to reveal only Jackson's red lace bra. For its part, MTV admits to a rehearsal that explored the possibility of a fake skirt being ripped away. Clearly, *something* was planned, even if it went awry. Jackson's subsequent apology, exonerating CBS and the NFL from any prior knowledge or guilt, hardly resolves the scandal. Nevertheless, on balance and regardless of whatever kind of stunt was planned in advance, the outcome favors Jackson. Not only does "Janet Jackson" become the most searched term in internet history, "Nipplegate" and "wardrobe malfunction" become household words.

6. Surprises can be learning moments, but often we refuse to learn from them. We're in denial. Unwilling to adapt to change, we try to thwart what's new.

Elvis Presley releases "Heartbreak Hotel" in 1956 and quickly becomes known as "the King." Frank Sinatra's response is to give a Tipper Gore like blast attacking rock and roll, describing it as "brutal, ugly, degenerate, vicious" and "sung, played and written, for the most part, by cretinous goons." The irony is that the same swooning of teenage girls for Presley that inspired this blast by Sinatra had, a decade earlier, been true of himself. If Sinatra is merely protecting his turf, he comes by his wide-eyed, ever-alert-to-danger instinct naturally. His mother Dolly is by all accounts his biggest childhood influence. Then one day, still wanting her son to grow up to become an aviation engineer, she notices a rival influence. There are now photos of the singer Bing Crosby adorning the teenager's bedroom, to which Dolly responds by throwing a shoe at her son.[8]

7. Other learning moments are embraced. We're open to how the world really works and respond by adjusting our internal forecasting model.

His pronouncements are legendary, beginning with "Float like a butterfly, sting like a bee." But others will surprise you. Consider: "The man who has no imagination has no wings" and "It isn't the mountains ahead to climb that wear you out; it's the pebble in your shoe." Nobody should underestimate Muhammad Ali, as the younger, stronger George Foreman discovers during the famous Rumble in the Jungle heavyweight championship bout held in Zaire in 1974. Showing his imagination, the 32-year-old Ali uses an unorthodox rope-a-dope strategy that requires taking endless punches to the gut in order to tire out Foreman, the prohibitive favorite.

That's Ali the boxer, but how about Ali the man? He's no fool, judging by his remark: "At home I am a nice guy, but I don't want the world to know. Humble people, I've found, don't get very far." Ali is drawing on what he's witnessed. His father had wanted to be a fine arts painter but ended up becoming a sign painter instead.[9] His son won't settle for anything less than realizing his own dreams. Attentive and concerned, with eyes that widen and inner eyebrows that frequently lift, Ali stretches his vision. "I'm something new," says the boxer who can rightly boast of being strong, proud, handsome, and witty, all at the same time.

Four Forms of Surprise

When we throw a surprise birthday party, we look closely to note just how pleasantly surprised the recipient is. Was the party a secret? Did the person suspect something was brewing? If that person's eyes don't go wide and mouth doesn't fall open, a smile alone isn't enough to confirm that a coup was pulled off.

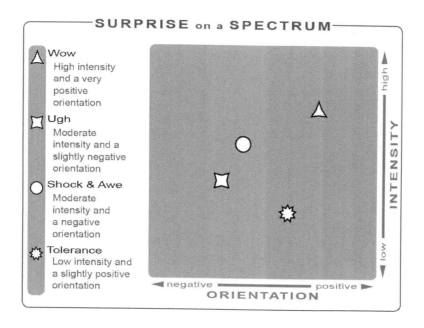

Three of the four forms of surprise revolve around what kind of emotional reaction accompanies or resolves the surprise. With a Wow surprise, it's joy. With the Tolerance version of surprise, it's the satisfaction or acceptance level of mild happiness that emerges. In contrast, an Ugh surprise involves some combination of the "negative" emotions of anger, sadness, disgust, and contempt. That leaves Shock & Awe—naked surprise—where a blatantly vulnerable quality predominates.

More specifically, each form of surprise gets shown as follows:

Wow: People who react with both joy and surprise are delighted by the unexpected. A big, true smile is joined by the eyebrows arching upwards, horizontal wrinkles appearing across the forehead, and the mouth fall-

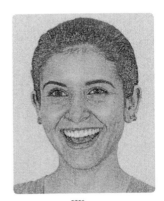

Wow

ing wide open to create a vertically stretched face. All but the forehead wrinkles are on display in the photo you see here. It's a fair bet that people who often emote in this way are likely to be full of enthusiasm and cheer.

Ugh: The opposite of Wow is Ugh, whereby people react to surprise with dismay. Any one or more of the so-called negative emotions of anger, sadness, disgust, and contempt will color their response. Large doses

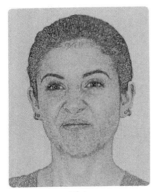

Ugh

of these emotions linked to surprise reveal uncomfortable responses to sudden changes in the status quo. The accompanying photo shows the raised outer eyebrows and open-eyed look of surprise combined with a raised upper lip favoring disgust.

Shock & Awe: The eyes go wide and the mouth drops open, exposing the teeth. The degree of the jaw drop can be modest, as evident in this case, or it can be more extreme instead. Intuitively, Shock & Awe signals people so caught off guard that they completely freeze. Of note is that with this form of surprise, the eyebrows *don't* rise (thus failing to aid vision and awareness). As a result, the look that emerges can suggest people stumbling along, rather than pro-actively adapting to change.

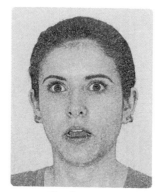

Shock & Awe

Tolerance

Tolerance: The inverse of Shock & Awe, Tolerance causes people to raise their eyebrows, taking in information, while they also manage satisfaction or acceptance smiles in reaction to what they've encountered. Tolerance suits people better able to accept and assimilate novelty. Anyone sporting this look will be more likely to believe that adapting to what's new is worth the effort, even if the smile is slight, as is true in this particular photo.

Each Form's Top 10 List

How do surprise's four forms apply to the celebrities facially coded for this book? While both Hollywood stars and musicians are consistently present, that's especially true in regards to the two more positively oriented forms: Wow and Tolerance. The celebrities who pop up on more than one of these four Top 10 lists are Marilyn Monroe, Little Richard, Walt Disney, and Caitlyn Jenner (with also an appearance by Bruce Jenner). Overall, female Hollywood stars are especially common here—as befits the unfortunate reality that in most scripts, even today, women are rarely the protagonists. Instead, they find themselves reacting to unexpected events foisted upon them.

Wow: Who but Walt Disney would sink to his knees on Main Street, all the better to appreciate how Disneyland's attractions are experienced from the vantage point of a six-year-old kid? Likewise, consider another example of Disney wanting to get the details right in order to create a wow. The Dodgers have moved to Los Angeles, and Goofy will throw out the first pitch in the team's new stadium. Disney insists on rehearsing the event until Goofy understands that to be *in-character*, he needs to be *incompetent*. As a result, Goofy realizes he must *bobble and drop* the ball the catcher tosses to him on the mound.

Wow

Marilyn Monroe
Little Richard
Ellen DeGeneres
Larry Page
Ingrid Bergman
Magic Johnson
Mary Lou Retton
Walt Disney
Frank Sinatra
Michael Jackson

In the Top 10 list for Wow are some of the most magnetic performers ever: Marilyn Monroe, Magic Johnson, and Michael Jackson. There is also a pair of businessmen. Like Walt Disney, Larry Page, Google's cofounder, tends to dream big. When fellow cofounder Eric Schmidt stepped down as CEO in 2011, he famously tweeted: "Day-to-day adult supervision no longer needed."[10] A spree of far-out projects and acquisitions have followed. While these efforts are casually referred to as "other bets" in investor relations documents, within Google they're known as "moonshots".

Ugh: From Timothy McVeigh and the Oklahoma City bombing to the Orlando nightclub shooting and the Sandy Hook massacre, the sense-less killings keep piling up. Once as shocking as any of those calamnities was when Charles Manson's followers murdered the actress Sharon Tate and four others in Los Angeles in 1969. According to Manson, in childhood he found himself sold by his mother for a pitcher of beer to a childless waitress, and an equally detached Manson showed no remorse while on trial for his role in the Tate killings.

TOP 10

Ugh

Edward R. Murrow
Jesse Jackson
Johnny Cash
Hillary Clinton
Aaron Rodgers
Alfred Hitchcock
Charles Manson
Elton John
Bill Cosby
Caitlyn Jenner

Infamy defines Manson, but not the others on this Top 10 list for Ugh. What everyone here does share is that in conjunction with surprise, they rarely link that feeling to happiness. For Johnny Cash, sadness often accompanies surprise. For Hillary Clinton and Aaron Rodgers, it's contempt; and so on.

In Elton John's case, when he feels surprise he typically also feels anger. As if to break that pattern, twice in February 2016 John created happy surprises. In London, he serenaded commuters at the St. Pancras railway station with a piano medley of his greatest hits. Then in Los Angeles, a free concert announced only the night before was staged in a parking lot. Which one? The lot that once belonged to a Tower Records store in which John often spent time perusing the latest releases.

Shock & Awe

Billy Graham
Bruce Jenner
Adele
Andy Warhol
Wayne Gretzky
Little Richard
Natalie Portman
Caitlyn Jenner
Jane Fonda
Michael Milken

Shock & Awe: Known to feel homesickness if on tour, Adele doesn't welcome surprises. Few singers would turn down an opportunity to perform the halftime show at a Super Bowl. For Adele, though, it was an easy decision to stay home because "I don't dance or anything like that."[11] Adele's song "Hello" is by her own account about "making it out alive from your late teens, early twenties,"[12] a look back that reflects the British diva's view of life as a harrowing, always on-the-edge-of-your-seat journey.

The Top 10 list for Shock & Awe is full of celebrities who frequently exhibit a version of surprise that may indicate somebody struggling to absorb and learn from their experiences. With two ministers on this list—Billy Graham and Little Richard—it's tempting to call the celebrities here *forever pilgrims*. There's often a bolt-from-the-blue, revelatory look to them that implies they retain some innocence, despite all their years of fame.

While everyone suffers bumps and bruises in life, several of these celebrities are notable for having undergone major changes. Wayne Gretzky merely changed the country he lived in as a hockey player, moving from Canada to America. Little Richard, however, went from rock star to minister; Jane Fonda from marrying the anti-war activist Tom Hayden to media mogul Ted Turner; and Bruce Jenner changed gender, appearing here twice (both as Bruce and Caitlyn). Rounding out this list: Michael Milken, a former junk bond king who has become a big-time philanthropist, giving support to medical research.

Tolerance: Mocking himself for his well-known shy ways, Jimmy Stewart would say of his marriage proposal to his first and only wife Gloria McLean: "I, I, I … pitched the big question to her last night and to my surprise she, she, she said yes!" That was 1949, and Stewart had recovered. Few know that in playing George Bailey in *It's a Wonderful Life* (1946), Stewart was under the influence. No, I'm not referring to booze. Stewart's newfound capacity for giving such a raw performance came amid recovery from post-traumatic stress following his service as a pilot in World War Two.

TOP 10

Tolerance

Estee Lauder
Aretha Franklin
John Lennon
Jimmy Stewart
Steven Spielberg
Jackie Onassis
Walt Disney
Marilyn Monroe
Paul McCartney
Elizabeth Taylor

The Top 10 list for Tolerance includes introverted celebrities like Jimmy Stewart, Steven Spielberg, and Jackie Kennedy Onassis. Then there's Estee Lauder, the only woman to make *Time* magazine's list of the 20 most influential business geniuses of the 20th century. She had once wanted to become an actress with her "name in lights" and her life a matter of "flowers and handsome men." If *settle* is the word, settle Lauder did, making a fortune from selling the beauty products her uncle, a chemist, initially developed.

Summary

Remember that anybody who looks surprised for more than a second is almost certainly faking it. Often, a third of a second or less: that's how quickly this emotion moves across the face. Triggered by a sudden, unexpected event, surprise hinges on the emotional verdict that follows. If no other emotion, positive or negative, mingles with, or follows close behind the *whoosh* of a surprise, then the unexpected proved to be of no real consequence—hence no additional feelings come into play.

Since it announces a change in the status quo, a surprise look merits our attention when we see it in others. There's probably an opportunity to seize, or a painful adjustment to make. Either way, with surprise our field of vision frequently widens to help us gather new information. Then it's encumbent on us to make the most of every new learning opportunity.

Fear

Catching on Fire

What Fear Means

Press conferences are a staple of quarterback Tom Brady's life. That makes it easy to compare Brady's facial expressions after a regular NFL game to his expressions amid the alleged football-tampering, Deflategate scandal. The difference between the quarterback's usual post-game facial expressions and those he shows during the scandal is vast.

Normally, Brady remains the epitome of unflappable. All kinds of smiles are commonplace. The guy has enjoyed plenty of success and it shows. Over two NFL seasons, I facially coded the first two minutes of press conferences given by every starting quarterback in the NFL, after both a winning and losing game. I chose which games based on the quarterback's performance being crucial to a given victory or loss. From that process, I typically covered four games per quarterback; and from that facial coding data, I can tell you the average NFL quarterback feels *twice as much fear* as Brady reveals during regular-season press conferences.

How about the Brady of the January 22, 2015 Deflategate press conference? Suddenly, he's ill at ease. He's showing five times more fear than in a press conference after a Patriots' loss. *Five times more fear* is a lot of fear. To look at Brady's mouth pulled anxiously wide, cheeks deflated, is to see a star quarterback severely out of his comfort zone.

For instance, during the Deflategate press conference, a reporter asks: "When and how did you supposedly alter the ball?" Even as the question is being asked, Brady swallows hard and the right side of his mouth stretches laterally, back towards the ear. Then as he answers, here's what happens: (mouth pulls wider) "I didn't" (mouth widens slightly more) "you know" (both eyebrows shoot upwards) "have any, uh ..." (mouth both widens again and falls open). "I didn't hold onto the balls in any way."

With a voice quavering at times, Brady will go on to offer other, not exactly on-point denials. One example is when he says, "I didn't alter the ball in any way," which Allysia Finley recasts in a *Wall Street Journal* opinion piece[1] as follows: "Of course, you didn't. Your ball boys did. That's what flunkies are for: Doing things you don't want to get caught doing and then taking the fall."

Similarly, note Brady's careful wording when asked if he had cheated: "I don't believe so. I feel like I've always played within the rules." On Bloomberg TV just a few minutes after the Deflategate press conference ends, what kind of appraisal do I give on the air? How culpable might Brady be? Seeking a point of reference, I cite an old Second City comedy skit. In it John Belushi is playing U.S. Senator Howard Baker during the Watergate hearings. "What I want to know," Belushi drawls, "is what did the President know and when did he *stop* knowing it?"

Awaiting not only the NFL's verdict, but also how public opinion will help to define his legacy, it's inevitable that Brady feels fear. This emotion is about being confronted by risk. Note how Finley adds, "Of course, you don't believe you did anything wrong." The question Brady is waiting to have answered the day of the press conference is, *now what will others believe*? In awaiting outcomes we can't control in life, we reactively experience fear as a submissive rather than dominant emotion. Facing threats that sometimes strike us as bigger than our ability to handle them, fear kicks in.

In general, fear is also an avoidance instead of an approach emotion. Other than safe, boredom-relieving exceptions like watching a scary movie or going on an amusement park ride, most people's basic orientation is *not* to approach a risk. When we're scared, more blood goes to the large muscles in our legs. It's as if nature is enabling us to run away, if we choose to do so, among the three basic options for handling fear: freeze, flight, or fight. In essence, when afraid we're driven to protect ourselves from uncertainty and possible harm. Fear is uncomfortable to feel or even contemplate feeling and, adventure-seekers aside, people typically hate to experience being on-edge for very long (if at all).

One final point here: the common, kneejerk impression of fear is that it's the worst of the "negative" emotions, especially for men. The male code is to be brave, impervious to fear. But of course both men and women experience fear. Anxiety and survival go hand in glove. Nothing is more important than being alert to danger so that we remain safe. As neuro-scientists have learned, within our brains our "fear button" (the amygdala) is also sensitive to monitoring other people's faces.[2] That makes sense given our ancient, instinctive concern about distinguishing between friend and foe by both identity and facial expressions alike.

Spotting Fear

A fearful face *opens* and may also blanch or tremble, as if someone afraid has "just seen a ghost." Like surprise, fear typically involves expressions that let us take in more information through widened eyes and lifted eyebrows. Compared to surprise, however, fear involves heightened tension and a more prolonged duration, indicating greater vigilance. The compression of facial muscles is stronger with fear because this emotion prepares us to confront likely danger. *Alarm* supersedes alertness, just as *fear* supplants surprise. More specifically, there is one tell-tale way in which fear is the singular emotion being shown:

Mouth & Chin

The lips pull back horizontally and become flattened, as does the skin above the chin.

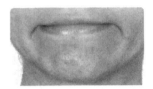

There are also five more ways fear gets expressed in conjunction with other core emotions:

Eyebrows

The inner part of one or both eyebrows lifts upwards, often creating forehead wrinkles.
(fear, sadness, surprise)

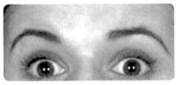

Eyebrows

The outer part of one or both eyebrows lifts upwards, often creating forehead wrinkles.
(fear, surprise)

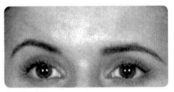

Eyebrows

The eyebrows come together and pull down, creating a vertical crease between the eyebrows.
(fear, anger, sadness)

Eyes

The eyes go wide as the upper eyelids rise.
(fear, anger, surprise)

Mouth & Jaw

The lips part and the jaw drops. Two degrees of response are shown here, moving from angular lip corners (upper photo) to an active stretching of the mouth that includes rounded corners and also the flattening and stretching of the cheeks and chin (lower photo). Whenever the mouth gets wider and stretches tightly, rather than remaining more relaxed, then this facial display interpretively favors fear over surprise.
(fear, surprise)

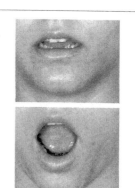

From the expressions just covered, it's obvious that fear and surprise often overlap. To distinguish between them, here are three tips for knowing when the emotion is likely to be fear, not surprise. First, look to see if both the inner and outer eyebrows are raised simultaneously. If that's true and the eyebrows are also taut and straight (rather than more gently rounded in shape), then the odds favor fear over surprise. Second, the odds again favor fear over surprise if the eyelids stay raised longer (rather than only very briefly). Third, the odds yet again favor fear over surprise if, when the mouth falls open, it's tense (rather than involving more relaxed lips).[3]

Fear's Top 10 List

After anger and sadness, fear is the third most versatile emotion in terms of the many ways it shows on people's faces. Fear also comes in third, far behind happiness and anger, in frequency. Among the celebrities analyzed for *Famous Faces Decoded*, on average almost 10% of their ex-

TOP 10

Most Fearful

Ronald Reagan
Wayne Gretzky
Natalie Portman
Marilyn Monroe
George H. W. Bush
Bill Cosby
Cam Newton
Jimmy Stewart
George W. Bush
Jackie Robinson

pressions involve fear. For the male celebrities in this book, the average amount of fear is higher, by a small but clear margin, than is true of their female counterparts.

The Top 10 list of the celebrities who are Most Fearful features such "manly men" sports stars as Wayne Gretzky, Cam Newton, and Jackie Robinson. (Not far off this Top 10 list appear other prominent athletes like Larry Bird, Willie Mays, Jack Nicklaus, and Muhammad Ali.) Also notable here is the White House pairing of Ronald Reagan and his vice president, George H. W. Bush. In contrast, there are just two women on this list. While Marilyn Monroe's source of alarm (childhood neglect) is crystal clear, Natalie Portman's remains obscure.

Finally, there's a special case. An aspect of fear is shyness: a social anxiety that makes people avoid saying or doing what they prefer. Extreme shyness affects an estimated 15% of Americans. Shyness may be why, for instance, Jimmy Stewart needed tutoring from Margaret Sullavan, the ex-wife of his best friend, Henry Fonda. Only then could Stewart keep his gawky, halting mannerisms from inhibiting his career.

Are there disadvantages to rarely feeling fear? Yes, there are because fear can help us maintain focus and gives us a jolt of energy helpful in tackling a challenge. Usually, however, there is more upside to eluding fear. People relatively free of this feeling won't tend to panic, be timid, or easily intimidated. While fear might motivate us, it's also true that remaining on "battle alert" for too long can cause chronic stress, which ultimately fatigues us.

Prominent on the Top 10 list for Least Fearful are two of the bold, self-promoting Kardhashian sisters: Khloe and Kim. The other four women on this list consist of a pair of hugely successful female business leaders, Martha Stewart and Estee Lauder; the billionaire author J. K. Rowling; and, intriguingly enough, Jennifer Aniston.

If the tabloids are to be believed, Aniston has been an emotional wreck seemingly *forever*. Although she played the role of a fairly neurotic

Least Fearful

Khloe Kardashian
J. K. Rowling
Kim Kardashian
Brian Jones
Martha Stewart
Jimmy Page
Estee Lauder
Bill Wyman
Jennifer Aniston
Bill Gates

Rachel Green on *Friends* (1994–2004), in real life Aniston emerges as among this book's least fearful celebrities. That result aligns with Aniston's approach to romance, which she has described in an interview as "Love just shows up and you go, 'Oh, wow, this is going to be a hayride and a half.'"[4] A low level of fear likewise fits the actresses's admission that whereas she "used to loathe confrontation,"[5] she no longer cringes like before.

How good are people at spotting fear? At 19%, this emotion ties disgust for having the lowest rate of accuracy detection. Despite the likely advantage of being aware of this emotion in others you may have to fight, detecting fear therefore appears not to be a commonly held skill. Among those in the Top 10 Most Fearful list, voters did reasonably well in recognizing that this emotion distinguishes these famous people only to the extent that their choosing surprise over fear for Ronald Reagan, George H. W. Bush, and George W. Bush constituted a near miss.

Otherwise, there's merely a single instance of voters getting it right. That would be Marilyn Monroe, for whom fear appears in both the voted and

Marilyn Monroe

Voted

sadness
fear

Actual

surprise
fear

Rare

anger

actual results. With Monroe, fear was evident in ways that often included a raised outer eyebrow and her mouth falling slightly ajar. Then again, fear by no means entirely gripped Monroe. When Joe DiMaggio wanted his new wife to become a quiet homemaker, the movie star refused to give up the limelight.[6] Instead, she filed for divorce from DiMaggio in 1954, citing "mental cruelty." An unintimidated Monroe also won her contract dispute with 20th Century Fox the next year, having objected to being both typecast and underpaid.

In contrast, Natalie Portman is among the Top 10 Most Fearful celebrities misjudged by voters as supposedly more distinguished by happiness. With this actress, fear typically reveals itself most clearly in how her eyes go wide and her mouth pulls wider. An understudy by age ten for the off-Broadway show *Ruthless!* (1992), Portman has said: "We all have phases of not feeling so great about ourselves." As I'll be discussing, the star of *Jackie* (2016) may in fact be her own worst critic.

Natalie Portman

Voted

happiness
happiness

Actual

fear
acceptance

Rare

satisfaction

What May Cause Fear

To describe fear as akin to catching on fire deliberately invites ambiguity. Both positive and negative connotations apply. The phrase's upside is that in sports or the fine arts arena, for instance, athletes or artists "catching on fire" are red-hot and doing well. They're in the flow, the zone; they're *feeling it*. Conversely, catching on fire is in the most literal sense a disaster. Your body is burning, and the adrenaline rush you feel is due to summoning your willpower to survive. As this list of six likely causes of fear will show, the risks involved include both physical and emotional danger.

1. We face a threat of physical pain, immediate or pending.

"Growing up, I was always the small guy," Wayne Gretzky recalls, a reality that forces him to be resourceful. At age six, his jersey hangs down so low his hockey stick gets caught in its hem as he skates around the rink. At age ten, Gretzky is a four-foot, four-inch tall center the season he scores an amazing 378 goals to go along with 120 assists. Nor are the physical threats confined to hockey rinks. Aware that teammates' parents feel their kids are being overshadowed by Gretzky's growing fame, a local baseball coach tells the youngster: "You won't live to see Christmas."

Even on turning pro in 1978, Gretzky finds the physical challenges never end. While he might be nicknamed The Great One, he's certainly not The Big One. He weighs 30 pounds less than the average NHL player. Whenever he and his Edmonton Oiler teammates have to take a strength test, Gretzky comes in dead last. To overcome those limitations, he skates to "where the puck is going to be" rather than where it is. Given the variety of ways he shows the emotion, most notably wide eyes and a mouth that stretches outward, it figures that Gretzky admits: "My whole sports life I've played in fear."[7]

2. We believe either grave physical or psychological harm is imminently possible, whether from our fellow human beings or otherwise.

Often wide-eyed, with inner eyebrows whose lift likewise indicates fear, Michael Phelps has had a nearly life-long inability to say the word "snake".[8] The back-story begins prior to Phelps's parents divorcing when he was nine years old. One day a young Phelps picks up a rock out in the yard and comes face-to-face with a hissing snake. Ever after, Phelps has suffered reoccurring nightmares involving snakes. Following an arrest for drunk driving in 2014, Phelps is now enrolled at a Phoenix-area trauma and addiction center. There, the swimmer comes to a realization: "whenever I was angry with my father or if anything about my father would come up, I'd have a dream about a snake that week."

Since his parents divorced, Phelps's interactions with his father Fred have been rare and almost always unsatisfying. Shaken by understanding the link between the nightmares and his dad, Phelps adds Fred to a list of guests welcome to visit him at the rehab clinic. Soon they're bonding (symbolically enough) over putting puzzles together. Coach Bob Bowman has always been Phelps's male mainstay. As the 2016 summer Olympics approach, Phelps suddenly has both his "dads" in his corner and feels mentally ready to become the most decorated Olympic athlete in history.

3. Psychological pain can include doubts that lead to self-loathing. Under pressure, we suffer through an internal drama.

Natalie Portman becomes a vegetarian by the age of eight, and while attending Harvard University tells *The New York Post*: "I don't care if [college] ruins my career. I'd rather be smart than a movie star." By then, Portman is already halfway through her participation in three *Star Wars* movies (1999, 2002, 2005). Of them, she says: "Everyone hated my performances" and "thought I was a terrible actress." This is no one-off instance of self-flagellation[9] from an actress whose signature expressions of fear involve her mouth pulling wide to match open-eyed looks. "I often feel insecure and don't believe in myself," Portman admits in a different media interview.

Where might Portman's "not feeling so great" about "almost every performance" of hers come from? The movie star's own words offer the best clues. That her family moved to America from Israel isn't everybody's experience in life, but seems rather benign. The same can't be said for the part of her childhood story where Portman confesses: "I have no clear memories from before I was around 12," and "I don't even remember who my friends were before I was nine."

Why might Portman's early childhood have been seemingly erased, at least within her own mind? A possible explanation emerges from Portman's reflection that as an only child, "You really learn to function as an adult." Could the stress of acting older than your age have been a factor in Portman's case? And how about the possible role of high expectations fostered early in life? Could demanding parents (perhaps her father, who's a well-published doctor) be behind Portman's admission that "Doubting yourself too much can also become like a sickness"? If so, then Portman's striving for excellence—even perfection—may explain her frequently harsh self-scrutiny.

4. The loss of social support from others, especially those we love, can leave us feeling deeply undermined.

From an unsettled childhood, what does Marilyn Monroe remember most painfully? That would be getting relegated by her mother, Gladys, in 1935 to the Los Angeles Orphans Home in Hollywood. There, the nine-year-old girl still known as Norma Jeane Mortenson vehemently protests: "But I'm not an orphan." Monroe's second husband, Arthur Miller, notes in his autobiography, *Timebends: A Life*, Monroe's "unrelenting uncertainty."[10] The fear she expresses most clearly by raising her outer eyebrows is a force Miller ultimately can't cope with any more than she can. As with her previous marriage to Joe DiMaggio, Monroe leaves Miller, too, and at age 36 is found dead of a barbiturate overdose.

5. A loss of status or power becomes a source of embarrassment for us and sets off alarm bells.

An estimated 95 million people are watching the world's suddenly most famous motor vehicle. A white Ford Bronco is being driven by a friend of O. J. Simpson as the ex-football star sits in the back seat, leading police on a low-speed chase along the #405 freeway in Los Angeles on June 17, 1994. Less well known[11] is that the evening before the chase, Simpson stays at the house of another friend: Robert Kardashian. From there the former running back nicknamed Juice escapes before the police can arrive. Left behind is what might have been a suicide note, which Kardashian reads on live TV in an apparent bid to garner support for his friend.

"I have nothing to do with Nicole's murder," Simpson has written. Kardashian then concludes by sharing with viewers the note's final words: "Don't feel sorry for me. I've had a great life, great friends. Please think of the real O. J. and not this lost person. Thanks for making my life special. I hope I helped yours. Peace and love. O. J."

What's changed in Simpson's life? His former wife Nicole Simpson is dead, her throat having been brutally slit. Nicole had left Juice, probably having taken up again with Marcus Allen, O. J.'s protégé, close friend, and somebody 15 years younger than himself and closer in age to Nicole. A friend of hers says Nicole's attitude was, *"You have lost me OJ. Watch me run."*[12] Now in the Bronco, the former running back has $8,000 in cash, a passport, a fake goatee, extra clothes, family photos of the children the former couple had together, and the .357 Magnum he's holding to his temple. What you can't see on TV is whether, once again, O. J.'s eyebrows are flashing upwards, as they so often do when he's feeling fear.

6. We face vague, unknown threats that endanger our future and leave us on unfamiliar, unsettled ground.

What must it feel like to be Jackie Robinson in his first MLB season in 1947? Given his many admirers, Robinson may not be the most hated man in the world, but he's certainly one of the most isolated. Film footage shows Robinson sitting alone in the Brooklyn Dodgers' dugout, eyes wide open, as he darts glances around the stadium as if alert to looming danger. By now he has already experienced plenty of abuse from bigots. First, Enos Slaughter tried to get his St. Louis Cardinals teammates to strike in protest of Robinson joining the league. Months later, Slaughter put a seven-inch gash in Robinson's leg by deliberately spiking the Dodgers' first baseman with his cleats on reaching the bag.

Where the next insult or threat will come from, Robinson never knows. His goal is to persevere with dignity. Not even all of his fellow players can be counted on. Putting down a brewing rebellion in the Dodgers' clubhouse, manager Leo Durocher curtly tells the squad (with no need to directly refer to Robinson): "I do not care if the guy is yellow or black, or if he has stripes like a fuckin' zebra. I'm the manager of this team, and I say he plays."

Four Forms of Fear

In general, the more a person's facial muscles stretch, the greater the likelihood you're witnessing somebody feeling fear. Now let's move to specifics. Like the Homeland Security Advisory System—with its color-coded terrorism threat levels from "low" (green) to "severe" (red)—what are the four forms of fear that identify various responses to experiencing duress?

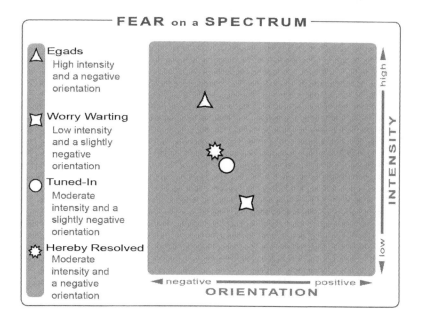

Fear expressions run the gamut from someone terrified (Egads); to concerned (Worry Warting); then merely watchful (Tuned-In); and finally, to a counter-response (Hereby Resolved). Of these fearful looks, Egads is utter fright. It's fear nakedly expressed. The other three forms feature an accompanying emotion that indicates the behavior likely to ensue. With Worry Warting, expect contemplation because sadness is also present. Tuned-In suggests a search for additional information because surprise figures prominently. Last but not least, Hereby Resolved is about fighting back against fear because the added emotion is anger.

More specifically, each form of fear gets shown as follows:

Egads: Really intense fear means you'll see people's eyes go wide and their lips pull back laterally, elongating the mouth. In this photo, the left outer eyebrow gets into the action by rising some, too. People who feel this degree of fear may not necessarily panic, however. Think

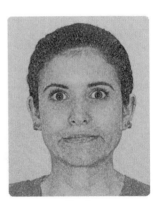

Egads

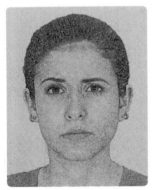

Worry Warting

of how animals often find value in freezing, hoping not to be noticed when a predator is lurking nearby.

Worry Warting: The inner eyebrows (normally) shoot upwards and simultaneously knit together, creating vertical wrinkles that form a crease. (In this case, little if any inner eyebrow lift is evident.) People prone to this look may fret without ever reducing, much less eliminating, the threat that caused it. These people may also be more susceptible than others to what is known in behavioral economics as *loss aversion*: a focus on potential losses, rather than gains, whenever a change occurs.

Tuned-In: Other times, people's eyebrows lift and their eyes go wide. Their lips also pull back horizontally. (The look on display here adds some sadness.) Safety is first on almost everyone's intuitive checklist, a frame of mind typified by the habit of glancing both ways before crossing the street. People who frequently show a Tuned-In expression honor the human tendency to doubt what's new and unfamiliar, and to accordingly remain hyperalert to danger as they make their way forward in life.

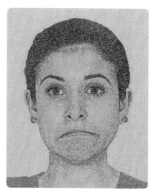

Tuned In

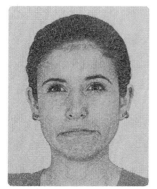

Hereby Resolved

Hereby Resolved: As striking as any mix of emotions is fear that incorporates anger. The fear part involves the lips pulling wide. The anger part can get expressed with firm lips, tightened lower eyelids, or even both of those displays at the same time. In this photo, taut eyelids take precedence over lips barely pressing together, if at all. The resulting look indicates the willingness to handle a threat. People who show this form of fear will most likely react to danger as if it's a speed bump. They might be slowed down, but odds are they won't be kept from moving ahead. If anything, they may even relish the excitement of a risky situation.

Each Form's Top 10 List

How do fear's four forms apply to the celebrities facially coded for this book? Across the board, Hollywood stars appear often. So do politicians and musicians, to a lesser extent. But while the Hollywood stars and musicians appear on all of the Top 10 lists about equally, the politicians are clustered within the two most negative forms of fear: Egads and Worry Warting. Jesse Jackson, Ronald Reagan, Natalie Portman, and Wayne Gretzky are the celebrities who put in more than one appearance across these lists, with female movie stars a common presence.

Egads: Jesse Jackson has often had an uneasy time of it in life. Experiences that have shaped him include: getting taunted by other kids regarding his out-of-wedlock birth; growing up under Jim Crow segregation laws in Greenville, South Carolina; and perhaps having Martin Luther King Jr. die in his arms (a claim disputed by King's other aides). "When we change the race problem into a class fight between the haves and the have-nots, then we are going to have a new ball game," Jackson observed in 1969, as he became King's heir apparent. Jackson's Rainbow Coalition solidified his stature thanks to respectable vote totals in running for president in 1984 and 1988. On the other hand, moments like calling New York City "Hymietown" and criticizing Barack Obama for "acting like he's white" have dented Jackson's stature.

Egads

Natalie Portman
Wayne Gretzky
Andy Warhol
Jane Fonda
Adele
Caitlyn Jenner
Billy Graham
Diana Ross
Joni Mitchell
Jesse Jackson

Intense fear cuts through the clutter like nothing else, and the anticipation of pain makes feeling fear worse. Among those on the Top 10 list for Egads is Jane Fonda. Her accomplishments range from award-winning movie roles to a series of best-selling exercise videos. Alongside those accomplishments, though, is a string of marriages to domineering men that has caused Fonda to wonder, "How was it that a seemingly strong woman could so thoroughly and repeatedly lose herself?"[13] Could the answer be found in Fonda's relationship with her father, Henry Fonda? "I would try to be perfect" Jane has written of her dad, who Katherine Hepburn described as "cold, cold, cold," after working with father and daughter to film *On Golden Pond* (1981).

Worry Warting: Pressed by a friend to articulate the overarching purpose of his prospective presidency in 1987, George H. W. Bush responded in exasperation: "Oh, the vision thing." More of a pragmatic caretaker by nature than a fierce partisan, Bush has said, "I have opinions of my own, strong opinions, but I don't always agree with them." Credit such modest hesitancy to the influence of Bush's patrician mother, who liked to remind him that nobody wanted to hear from the *Great I Am.*[14] Pulling together a coalition to fight the Iraq War was quintessential Bush. His childhood nickname was *Have-Half,* due to his preference for building social ties by splitting any candy or other treats evenly with friends.

> **TOP 10**
> ## Worry Warting
> George H. W. Bush
> Humphrey Bogart
> Yogi Berra
> Jay-Z
> Marlon Brando
> Cary Grant
> Jackie Robinson
> Clint Eastwood
> Ronald Reagan
> George W. Bush

The Top 10 list for Worry Warting is at times a matter of one-degree-of-separation from George H. W. Bush. Both his son George and the president he served under (Ronald Reagan) join him here. This entirely-male list showcases many contemplative, even brooding types. Outside of politics, note the inclusion of a pair of athletes from baseball: a sport that gives you plenty of time to think.

Tuned-In: One manifestation of Tuned-In fits Ingrid Bergman perfectly, even if she didn't quite qualify for this list. Prone to raised outer eyebrows that gave her a wary look, the actress was no stranger to sensing danger, whether social or spiritual in nature. These days Bergman's scandal seems quaint. The married heroine of movies like *Notorious* (1946) was denounced on the floor of the U.S. Senate in 1950 for bearing a child out of wedlock with Italian film director Roberto Rossellini. Why the romantic spark? Bergman admired Rossellini's daring work at a time when both her marriage to a dentist

> **TOP 10**
> # Tuned-In
> **Wayne Gretzky**
> **Bill Cosby**
> **Edward R. Murrow**
> **Marilyn Monroe**
> **Jesse Jackson**
> **Frank Sinatra**
> **Larry Ellison**
> **Jimmy Stewart**
> **Little Richard**
> **Natalie Portman**

and the roles she was being offered in Hollywood felt stifling. Described by producer David O. Selznick as "the most completely conscientious actress" he ever had the pleasure to work with, Bergman could be wary but not craven. By 1950 she had already played a nun and a virgin saint on screen, building an image strong enough to keep the public rooting for her despite the scandal.

In the Top 10 list for Tuned-In appears a new name that may best give you the spirit of this look: Larry Ellison. He's a two-time college dropout who, in getting ahead, saw threats to his success lurking everywhere. At least once, a sign of the animosity the rapacious, ever-on-guard Ellison has spurred by trash-talking about competitors was *literally* a sign. A business rival of Ellison's had a "Caution Dinosaur Crossing" street sign installed near the offices of Ellison's company, Oracle, during the 1990s, invoking Silicon Valley's most dreaded put-down: you're obsolete.[15]

Hereby Resolved: Certainly more given to anger than fear, Tom Brady is nevertheless an exemplary example of Hereby Resolved on a recent occasion. "Let's go! Let's show some fight! Let's play harder! Harder! Tougher! Everything!" That's what Brady was yelling on the sidelines to his teammates when they were down 28-3 in Super Bowl 51.[16] Never had the 39-year-old Brady taken so many line-of-scrimmage snaps in a game (99) as he did against the Atlanta Falcons. Overcoming the biggest deficit in Super Bowl history on the

> **TOP 10**
> # Hereby Resolved
> Douglas MacArthur
> Eminem
> John Bonham
> Ronald Reagan
> Leonardo DiCaprio
> Angelina Jolie
> Khloe Kardashian
> Sandra Bullock
> Robert Redford
> Kanye West

way to his fifth championship ring, Brady didn't choke. When cornered, he fought off the threat of losing with incredible composure.

Among the Top 10 list for Hereby Resolved, let's focus on two examples of grit and fortitude. In reviewing the movie *Gravity*, a reporter for *The New York Times* calls Sandra Bullock "arguably Hollywood's gutsiest A-list actress."[17] Similarly, what does Peggy Noonan believe was Ronald Reagan's defining characteristic? Courage. While trailing Gerald Ford for the 1976 Republican nomination, Reagan tells his staff: "I don't care if I lose every damn primary" prior to taking the fight with Ford to the party's convention. Noonan remembers that moment as confirming Reagan's "warmly ruthless" nature.[18]

Summary

It's time to retire the pejorative notion that feeling fear means you're a "spineless wimp." The emotion's impact isn't so certain. Facing a threat can either arm or disarm people, depending on however they handle the challenge. The prospect of pain causes some people to tackle a situation, whereas others avoid even acknowledging discomfort. Social support can make a difference as to which course of action people follow.

An affirmative example of fear spurring on greatness is the story of Muhammad Ali, the former heavy-weight boxing champion of the world. For Ali, *running scared* got transformed into dancing around the ring. What did Ali dread?[19] In the summer of 1955, his dad showed him photographs of Emmett Till's mutilated corpse. That African-American teenager from Chicago had been lynched after supposedly whistling at a white woman in a grocery store while visiting cousins in Mississippi. Ali would later recall lying "awake scared, thinking about somebody getting cut up or being lynched." Soon a white policeman coaching at a nearby gym turned Ali's thoughts to boxing instead. From that suggestion, Ali's dread was eclipsed by a new reality: Ali dominating his chosen profession in a way that made "Black Power" awe-inspiring to watch.

Epilogue

Lying

Can You Spot Deceit?

In the comedy *Liar, Liar* (1997), Jim Carrey stars as a self-aggrandizing, dishonest Los Angeles lawyer. His ashamed son asks, as a birthday wish, for his dad to stop lying for a day. Instantly, that wish comes true and the lawyer begins blurting out all sorts of offensive, painful truths certain to destroy both his career and private life.

In reality as opposed to a movie, it's estimated that 42% of people tell up to five lies a day and 11% of us over five lies daily.[1] Those are just the lies known to us, the lies we tell *others*. What about the lies we're only dimly, half-aware of telling *ourselves*?[2] (Examples might range from "What's the harm of taking home some of my company's office supplies?" to "My spouse starts all the fights.") If those private lies—sometimes the biggest lies—are included, the actual amount of lying could be much higher. After all, people are like a fun house of mirrors. We embody our own contradictions. We're not bred to be truth machines because our top priorities in life are to attract allies (survival) and to feel good about ourselves (pleasure).[3]

As Carrey's *Liar, Liar* predicament illustrates, lying isn't always bad any more so than the "negative" emotions covered in *Famous Faces Decoded* are always bad. Polite lies can douse the flames of what could otherwise be a lot of contentious encounters with people. Overall, though, as little as 7% of the lies we tell are considered to be altruistic. In comparison, 44% of them are meant to promote ourselves and another 34% are meant to protect us. (The other 13% of our lying reflects ambiguous motives, maliciousness, or even pathological dishonesty.[4])

From the other perspective, being the deceived party rarely, if ever, feels good—*especially* if the stakes are high. Many lies involve important information that's been hidden or diverted away from us. Remember Oprah Winfrey's outrage on finding out that one author she was championing, James Frey, had made up much of his memoir? As we try to size up others, knowing whether we're dealing with a "liar" or not is of vital interest to us. The number one question I get asked after a speech has long been: does knowing facial coding mean you can "tell when people are lying?"

If only it were that simple.

There is no single facial muscle movement or signature expression that betrays a lie. If there were, believe me, somebody would have "bottled it" by now. Law enforcement officers, oversight committees, and suspicious spouses would all have an easier time confirming or disproving their doubts than is actually the case. That said, some clues exist.

Possible Tells

You might think the surest way to spot lying is to look for fear. You're only partially correct. Habitual liars or simply very good liars may not show any fear, or show it so subtly you won't notice. In this camp are liars who believe their own lies *are* the truth, making those instances among the hardest ones to detect.

Then again, there's Richard Nixon—a terrible liar. In 1977, an often fearful Nixon sat down with David Frost for a series of interviews that inevitably focused on the Watergate scandal. The footage reveals Nixon's eyelids nervously fluttering, his voice quavering at times, and plenty of faltering word choices. But it's how often and strongly Nixon's outer eyebrows shoot up, and how much his mouth pulls wide as he insists there wasn't a cover-up, that should draw your attention. Nixon's face is spontaneously *leaking* the truth. The guy is profoundly uncomfortable with many of the assertions he's making in giving his version of the scandal, including most famously: "When the President does it, that means that it's not illegal."

Despite Nixon's example, more than fear should be on your radar screen in trying to spot a liar. Let's cover the other emotions, starting with anger. Self-righteous indignation is a technique often resorted to by people engaged in lying, as in *how dare you impugn my integrity.*

When interviewed at length by Oprah Winfrey in 2013, a combative Lance Armstrong showed almost no fear but often two of anger's four forms: Thunderstorm and Battle Ready. Yes, the seven-time Tour de France cycling champion was no longer maintaining that he had "never doped." Despite his new-found honesty, however, Armstrong wasn't backing down much during the interview. He remained angry and defiant in answering Winfrey's questions, painting himself as unfairly persecuted in a sport awash with fellow cheaters and hypocritical reformers pursuing their own agendas.

Alongside fear and anger, another emotion sometimes implicated in lying is sadness. Typically in these cases, the liars are disappointed in themselves for engaging in deception. In 1960, an American U-2 spy plane was shot down over the Soviet Union. President Dwight Eisenhower's administration initially denied having engaged in espionage, calling the CIA plane a NASA aircraft and releasing a photograph of a U-2 plane repainted in NASA's colors. But when the Russians let it be known that they had the pilot, Gary Powers, in captivity, Eisenhower then belatedly gave a face-saving, tell-*some* (not all) press conference. A mixture of hesitant words and sadness-laden signals followed, with Eisenhower saying America had now "uh" (a long pause, head down, and a wince) "publicly admitted" (eyes lowering) "that the U-2 belonged to us and was on a reconnaissance mission" (head drooping again). Then the anguish Eisenhower felt in private[5] about having lied became obvious for all to see.

Contempt (and occasionally disgust) can likewise figure into a lie. When you don't respect yourself for lying or, instead, don't respect who you're lying to, contempt may make an appearance. Here again, Eisenhower serves as an example because he also smirked during the passage just cited. Given that sadness was accompanying a sign of contempt, odds are good that a dejected Eisenhower also disrespected *himself* for lying.

In contrast, consider the case of Bernie Madoff. Arrested in 2008 for bilking investors like Steven Spielberg, Sandy Koufax, and Zsa Zsa Gabor out of a combined $65 billion—based on promising them steady, eye-popping returns that defied reason—Madoff is likely an example of people who easily lie to others they denigrate as gullible.

What might merit that conclusion? Two details are noteworthy in regards to Madoff's emoting. First, he's prone to combining a smirk with a smile. In those cases, one side of the upper lip rises more quickly, reaches higher, and comes down more slowly than the other, smiling lip corner. That smile-and-smirk combination is often the mark of relishing one's scorn of others. Second, when not showing that combination, Madoff usually has a poker face. There's little to no emotion shown, worrisome in itself because our emotions most reliably turn on *when* we *care about others*, including how they feel about us.

The good news about lie detection is that the so-called negative emotions I've just discussed are hard for most people to fake.[6] The bad news is that anger aside, the other "negative" emotions of fear, sadness, contempt, and disgust don't occur frequently. Moreover, those five emotions, including anger, often get *squelched* in social settings. That verb refers to when people try to suppress a reaction they suspect they're showing, or else quickly deploy a social smile to either cover up a negative feeling or soften a snide comment.

What's the next best fallback if spotting "negative" emotions doesn't help catch a liar? Once again, don't rely on words. Always remember the Russian leader Joseph Stalin's cynical observation: A "diplomat's words must have no relations to actions.... Sincere diplomacy is no more possible than dry water or iron wood."

A better approach to lie detection is to broaden your focus to include smiles, most notably satisfaction-level "social smiles." Those polite smiles may mask true feelings. Throw a smile on your face and you've made happiness into a commodity. The always-smiling, whether feeling happy or not character of Smiler in *The Emoji Movie* (2017) is a case in point. Smiles can defuse anger and relieve sadness—and constructively so. Smiles may, however, also become a tool for manipulation and outright deception.

To explore smiles (meant to deceive others) more deeply, we need to consider terms like *onset* and *offset* as well as *duration*.[7] As my sidebar chart on the next page illustrates, the usual smile—and indeed any natural expression—should have timing that resembles a wave hitting the shore. Look for the expression to rise, have a peak, then break and dissipate. As a cheat sheet to help you spot a lie or merely somebody faking a feeling of happiness, here are some tips for when smiles are part of the action.

Oddly Timed Smiles: With inauthentic emoting, it's hard to get the timing right. In my chart's pair of diagrams, entitled the Timing of True & Fake Smiles, notice the rhythm of the three separate stages of an expression (which often unfold within a four-second duration or less):

- The onset stage of a true smile can instead become the launch pad for an abrupt fake smile—namely, a fake *Light Bulb Smile*. This kind of smile turns on with unnatural speed and brightness. Example: In the 2012 vice presidential debate, a folksy Joe Biden offered up so many sudden, flashing grins that pundits and viewers alike doubted their veracity. Then four years later, a smiling Biden was asked by a reporter (after meeting with the new Vice President:) "Are you smiling right now because you genuinely like Mike Pence?" Biden's reply, "No, I'm not," reinforced the idea that not all of Biden's quick-to-flash grins are genuine.[8]

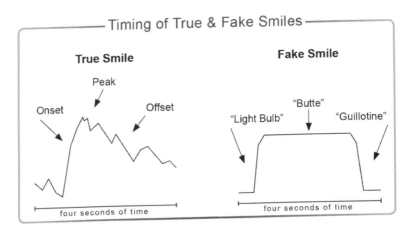

- The peak stage of a true smile can instead become a bulldozed mountaintop that signals a fake smile. A fake *Butte Smile* forgoes a peak of greatest intensity in favor of a flat-topped, overly long smile. Example: I've called Mitt Romney the Energizer Bunny of Social Smiles because his smooth, even unctuous smiles tend to go on *and on*, well past the more natural outer limit of one to two seconds of sustained intensity.

- The offset stage of a true smile can instead become the all-too-sudden closing act of a fake smile—namely, a fake *Guillotine Smile* that's here, then gone, rather than naturally fading away. This type of fake smile takes its name from the way a guillotine blade makes a rapid descent. Example: When Rachel Dolezal, the NAACP's Spokane, Washington chapter president, was exposed as actually being white in June of 2015, she was interviewed by Matt Lauer. During the segment, her every smile quickly ebbed in response to yet another probing question.[9]

Directly Contradicted Smiles: A second way to look for suspect smiles is when a display of happiness is contradicted by its opposite emotion, namely, sadness. During an *Embarrassed Smile*, people's smiles intensify at *exactly* the same time that their heads pitch down and tilt one way or the other in a sign of slumping sadness. Example: A very modest version of this look came during Ronald Reagan's Oval Office address on the Iran-Contra Affair. Just after a slightly smiling Reagan hid behind the excuse that he hadn't been kept "fully informed" about the goings-on within his own administration, he broke eye contact with the camera, looking sheepishly down at his notes.[10]

Incongruous Smiles: Finally, there are three types of incongruous smiles that lack consistency:

- The classic, words-based version of incongruity is the *Say-Feel Gap Smile*. In these cases, a sign of potential lying is that what the person is saying doesn't fit the emoting. You might hear "I'm so relieved," but you're seeing fear or sadness linger on the person's face. Example: Ohio governor John Kasich may be as honest as any politician around, but often times while Kasich's message is hopeful, his dour, "barbed-wire" smiles suggest his dreams for America will be hard to achieve.

- The physical version of incongruity is the *Lopsided Smile*. In these cases, the smile will be uneven across the face. Such smiles give the appearance of having been *willed* onto the face, as a self-conscious display that everything is supposedly fine with the speaker. Example: Many a carved pumpkin ends up with a crooked smile. Here, notice how the smile is slightly higher on the right side.

Lopsided Smile

- Perhaps most intriguing is the subtle, psychological version of incongruity,[11] which could be called the *Cookie Jar Smile*. These people have been caught with their hands in a cookie jar, so to speak, but they're so pleased with themselves that you just know they'll be back for more. Example: As the Whitewater investigation morphed into a probe of his affair with Monica Lewinsky, Bill Clinton found himself deposed under oath. Asked if it was true that "there is no sexual relationship" between Lewinsky and himself, Clinton gave a slight smile and a little tug on his lower lip, a small sign of defiance, in replying that his answer "depends on what your definition of 'is' is."

Caution in Drawing Conclusions about People

Facial coding provides a strong, viable opportunity to gauge others through the actions evident on their faces, and on-going usage will make the tool ever sharper in your own hands. Nevertheless, remember that facial coding can tell you what people are *feeling* at a specific moment in time, but not what they're *thinking*. It's a tool to be utilized carefully. Anyone who promises you can "speed read" others, quickly profiling them, is being entirely too facile. Yes, you can use facial coding to gauge somebody's emotions in the moment and, *over time*, look for patterns. But context matters, with multiple and seemingly contradictory impulses and emotions frequently involved.

To quote the Danish philosopher Soren Kirkegaard: "Out of the twisted timber of humanity, no straight thing was ever made." People are complicated, so take into account of the "knots" in the wood and don't rush to judgment. Nobody needs a return to the 19th and early 20th century physiognomy movement,[12] when an emphasis on *fixed* facial *features* (like hooked noses) aided and abetted racism.

In contrast, facial coding is at its heart about flexibility, humanity, and seeking better, sustained rapport with others in your professional and personal life. As I have shown in *Famous Faces Decoded*, even with happiness (the simplest of the emotions in terms of its display), variety exists along a continuum regarding the strength of a smile and the four forms of expression possible. There is no single template per emotion but, rather, diverse ways in which facial coding's seven core emotions get shown, with often two or more emotions being signaled by a look.

Furthermore, there are many instances involving the 173 celebrities in this book where emotionally complex people tend to show two contradictory emotions at the same time. Such people aren't easily classified, nor should they be. To call them "two-faced" (liars) would be an injustice.

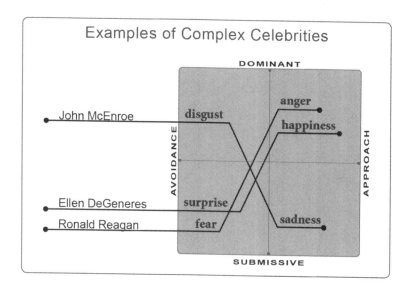

At times, someone's most characteristic emotions may land in opposing places on the dimensions of *approach* versus *avoidance* and *dominant* versus *submissive*. Notice how in John McEnroe's case, for instance, feeling disgust means he's pulling away at the same time that he longs to be hugged, given the sadness he often also feels. Those two emotions fall in opposite quadrants, creating an inevitable tension. Ellen DeGeneres, in turn, is sparklingly happy yet remains alert to whatever may change quickly around her, given her propensity for surprise. As to Ronald

Reagan's expressions, his two most characteristic emotions were fear and anger. While Reagan "came on strong," exhibiting lots of anger, he may well have been trying to override an underlying sense of insecurity that simultaneously caused him to feel fear.

Recognizing and relating well to individuals with complex emotions stands in contrast to resorting to terms like "hot head," "sad sack," and "chicken". Those epithets are one-dimensional, pejorative ways of describing people who tend to feel anger, sadness, and fear, respectively, and need to be replaced by a richer, more nuanced, and empathetic approach. My use of four forms per emotion is, by comparison, meant to give you, my reader, an easy handle by which to grasp the emotional nuances involved, without devolving into stereotypes.

In *Famous Faces Decoded*, I've tried to take you through the journey I started two decades ago. Sure, I knew terms like "happiness" or "anger (management)." Up until that point in my life, however, I hadn't realized that emotions could be examined systematically or that a visual playbook existed for spotting them in others.

People can be fascinating or frustrating, depending on circumstance. What remains consistent is that by using emotional intelligence to navigate situations in life, we'll benefit from a feedback loop. Only then can we get out of our own heads and into the hearts of others. Thanks to facial coding, a means exists to understand what people are feeling and how they're responding to us. Even better, with practice that feedback loop can operate spontaneously, right in the moment, when it's not too late to adjust our behavior and achieve a better outcome.

There's a wealth of great quotes that could be relevant to applying the learnings available in this book. Henry James's adage, "Never say you know the last word about any human heart," comes to mind. So does Yogi Berra saying, "You can observe a lot by just watching." But I decided to open

Famous Faces Decoded by invoking a trio of less familiar quotes by Oscar Wilde, George Orwell, and Erica Jong instead.

People's tendency to see without seeing informs Wilde's remark. His reference to *appearances* isn't an endorsement of physiognomy or merely a nod to matters like clothing style and grooming. After all, Wilde's lone novel deals with how our recurring experiences in life both inform and alter our feelings. Orwell's quote gets more specific, pointing out how the sum of our previous experiences can leave their imprint on our faces due to muscle memory.

Finally, Jong echoes James's adage by noting how poorly we comprehend others, no matter how famous. Hardly anything is truly known in life. Facial coding serves to shed some light, as dim as that or any light may be, given the difficult and on-going goal of understanding people—ourselves included.

WHAT EMOTIONS MEAN

"POSITIVE" EMOTIONS	DISPLAY	MEANING	UPSIDE	DOWNSIDE
JOY (strongest happiness)	big smile, eyes twinkle	*happiness* robust fulfillment	creative, open-minded	too carefree, unfocused
PLEASURE (2nd-level happiness)	big smile			
SATISFACTION (3rd-level happiness)	slight smile	happiness modest fulfillment	appreciative, receptive	hold back, fail to embrace
ACCEPTANCE (4th-level happiness)	smile hint			

NEUTRAL EMOTION	DISPLAY	MEANING	UPSIDE	DOWNSIDE
SURPRISE	face elongates	attentive	alert, on-guard	hesitant, puzzled

"NEGATIVE" EMOTIONS	DISPLAY	MEANING	UPSIDE	DOWNSIDE
ANGER	face contracts	lack control, hit back	assertive, solve problems	hot-headed, resentful
FEAR	face opens	at risk, discomfort	self-protective	freeze, choke
SADNESS	face wrinkles	irrevocable loss	empathetic, reflective	feel helpless, lose hope
DISGUST	face recoils	rejection	avoid "poison"	overly detached
CONTEMPT	smirk	superiority, disrespect	confident	isolated, dismissive

Comprehensive Results

Presented here are all of the **Voted** survey results and the **Actual** facial coding results. Voted results came from a market research survey conducted in late 2016. Actual results came from a research study of those same celebrities via facial coding, thereby making comparisons possible.

Name	Highest Voted	2nd Voted	Highest Actual	2nd Actual	Rare
Hank Aaron	*Happiness*	Happiness	Disgust	Contempt	Acceptance
Adele	*Happiness*	Happiness	Disgust	Sadness	Satisfaction
Muhammad Ali	Anger	Happiness	Surprise	Fear	Acceptance
Woody Allen	Sadness	Surprise	Surprise	Fear	*Pleasure*
Jennifer Aniston	Happiness	*Happiness*	Satisfaction	*Joy*	Fear
Neil Armstrong	*Happiness*	Happiness	Contempt	Sadness	Surprise
Ingrid Bergman	Happiness	Sadness	Surprise	Fear	Anger
Yogi Berra	*Happiness*	Surprise	*Pleasure*	Sadness	Anger
Chuck Berry	Happiness	Sadness	Satisfaction	Surprise	Disgust
Beyonce (Knowles)	*Happiness*	Happiness	*Joy*	Acceptance	Contempt
Jeff Bezos	*Happiness*	Contempt	Sadness	Surprise	Acceptance
Larry Bird	*Happiness*	Happiness	Fear	Surprise	Contempt
Humphrey Bogart	Sadness	Anger	Fear	Sadness	Satisfaction
Barry Bonds	Anger	Sadness	Disgust	*Joy*	Satisfaction
John Bonham	*Happiness*	Anger	Anger	Acceptance	Surprise
Tom Brady	Happiness	*Happiness*	Contempt	*Pleasure*	Acceptance
Marlon Brando	Happiness	Sadness	Sadness	Fear	*Pleasure*
Garth Brooks	Happiness	*Happiness*	Acceptance	Contempt	Sadness
Sandra Bullock	*Happiness*	Happiness	Acceptance	Anger	Sadness
George H. W. Bush	Happiness	Surprise	Fear	Sadness	Satisfaction
George W. Bush	Happiness	Surprise	Fear	Contempt	Satisfaction
Jeb Bush	Sadness	Anger	Satisfaction	Anger	Fear
Mariah Carey	Happiness	Sadness	*Pleasure*	*Joy*	Anger
Johnny Cash	Happiness	Contempt	Sadness	Anger	Satisfaction
Cher	Surprise	Happiness	Acceptance	Surprise	*Joy*
Julia Child	*Happiness*	Happiness	*Joy*	*Pleasure*	Contempt
Roger Clemens	Happiness	Anger	Disgust	Anger	Fear
Patsy Cline	Happiness	Sadness	*Pleasure*	Satisfaction	Fear
Bill Clinton	Surprise	Happiness	Sadness	Disgust	Acceptance
Hillary Clinton	Happiness	Anger	Sadness	Contempt	Acceptance
Kurt Cobain	Sadness	Anger	Anger	Sadness	*Joy*
Bill Cosby	Sadness	Anger	Surprise	Fear	Acceptance
Ray Croc	Surprise	Happiness	Satisfaction	*Pleasure*	Disgust
Walter Cronkite	Happiness	Anger	Acceptance	Satisfaction	Disgust
Tom Cruise	Surprise	Happiness	Anger	Contempt	Acceptance
Bette Davis	*Happiness*	Happiness	Surprise	Acceptance	Contempt
Robert De Niro	Anger	Happiness	Sadness	Fear	*Pleasure*
James Dean	Anger	Sadness	Sadness	Anger	Disgust
Ellen DeGeneres	*Happiness*	Happiness	*Joy*	*Pleasure*	Sadness

Name	Highest Voted	2nd Voted	Highest Actual	2nd Actual	Rare
Princess Diana	Sadness	Fear	Acceptance	Anger	Disgust
Leonardo DiCaprio	Happiness	*Happiness*	Anger	Acceptance	Surprise
Joe DiMaggio	*Happiness*	Happiness	Surprise	Contempt	Disgust
Walt Disney	*Happiness*	Surprise	Surprise	Satisfaction	Anger
Bob Dylan	Anger	Sadness	Anger	*Pleasure*	Fear
Clint Eastwood	Anger	Happiness	Contempt	Fear	Surprise
Dwight Eisenhower	Happiness	Surprise	Contempt	Sadness	Acceptance
Larry Ellison	Happiness	Disgust	Surprise	Satisfaction	Acceptance
Eminem	Anger	Contempt	Anger	Fear	Satisfaction
Jane Fonda	Happiness	*Happiness*	Acceptance	Fear	Anger
Jodie Foster	Happiness	Surprise	Acceptance	Contempt	Sadness
Aretha Franklin	Happiness	Sadness	Acceptance	Satisfaction	Disgust
Joe Frazier	Anger	Disgust	Surprise	Fear	Acceptance
Judy Garland	Sadness	Happiness	*Pleasure*	Satisfaction	Anger
Bill Gates	Happiness	*Happiness*	Contempt	Satisfaction	Fear
Billy Graham	Happiness	*Happiness*	Fear	*Pleasure*	Acceptance
Cary Grant	Happiness	Surprise	Sadness	Fear	Satisfaction
Wayne Gretzky	Happiness	*Happiness*	Fear	Surprise	Contempt
Tom Hanks	*Happiness*	Happiness	Anger	Fear	*Pleasure*
George Harrison	Happiness	Sadness	*Pleasure*	Satisfaction	Acceptance
Hugh Hefner	*Happiness*	Happiness	Satisfaction	Contempt	Surprise
Jimi Hendrix	Surprise	Sadness	Anger	Contempt	*Pleasure*
Jim Henson	Happiness	*Happiness*	*Joy*	Satisfaction	Anger
Audrey Hepburn	Happiness	*Happiness*	Acceptance	Fear	Anger
Katharine Hepburn	Happiness	*Happiness*	*Joy*	*Pleasure*	Contempt
Alfred Hitchcock	Surprise	Fear	Surprise	Fear	Satisfaction
Dustin Hoffman	Happiness	*Happiness*	Acceptance	Anger	Satisfaction
Whitney Houston	Sadness	Fear	*Pleasure*	Disgust	Anger
Janet Jackson	Surprise	Happiness	Fear	*Joy*	Anger
Jesse Jackson	Anger	Disgust	Surprise	Fear	Acceptance
Michael Jackson	Sadness	Fear	Surprise	Fear	Anger
Mick Jagger	*Happiness*	Happiness	*Joy*	Surprise	*Pleasure*
LeBron James	*Happiness*	Happiness	Disgust	Sadness	Satisfaction
Bruce Jenner	Surprise	Happiness	Satisfaction	*Pleasure*	Disgust
Caitlyn Jenner	Surprise	Happiness	Surprise	Fear	Contempt
Steve Jobs	Surprise	Sadness	Anger	Surprise	Sadness
Elton John	Happiness	Sadness	Acceptance	Anger	*Joy*
Magic Johnson	Happiness	*Happiness*	*Joy*	*Pleasure*	Anger
Angelina Jolie	Anger	Sadness	Acceptance	Anger	*Pleasure*
Brian Jones	Happiness	*Happiness*	Satisfaction	Contempt	Fear
Janis Joplin	Sadness	Anger	Sadness	*Joy*	Anger
Jay-Z (Carter)	*Happiness*	Contempt	Sadness	Fear	Satisfaction
Michael Jordan	*Happiness*	Surprise	Disgust	Fear	Satisfaction
Jackie Joyner-Kersee	*Happiness*	Surprise	*Pleasure*	*Joy*	Contempt
Khloe Kardashian	Sadness	Happiness	Anger	Acceptance	Fear

Name	Highest Voted	2nd Voted	Highest Actual	2nd Actual	Rare
Kim Kardashian	Happiness	Surprise	Satisfaction	Contempt	Fear
Kourtney Kardashian	Happiness	Sadness	Acceptance	Anger	Fear
Diane Keaton	Happiness	*Happiness*	*Joy*	Satisfaction	Anger
J. Kennedy (Onassis)	Happiness	Surprise	Surprise	Satisfaction	Sadness
John F. Kennedy	Happiness	Surprise	Satisfaction	Sadness	Surprise
Robert F. Kennedy	Happiness	*Happiness*	Sadness	Acceptance	Contempt
Billie Jean King	Happiness	Surprise	Disgust	*Joy*	Acceptance
Martin Luther King	Anger	Happiness	Fear	Surprise	Disgust
Estee Lauder	Happiness	*Happiness*	Satisfaction	Acceptance	Sadness
Jennifer Lawrence	Happiness	*Happiness*	Acceptance	*Joy*	Fear
John Lennon	Happiness	Sadness	Satisfaction	*Pleasure*	Anger
David Letterman	Happiness	Surprise	*Joy*	Contempt	Surprise
Rush Limbaugh	Anger	Contempt	Anger	Disgust	Fear
Douglas MacArthur	Disgust	Contempt	Anger	Acceptance	Satisfaction
Bernie Madoff	Anger	Contempt	Acceptance	Sadness	Satisfaction
Madonna	Happiness	*Happiness*	Acceptance	*Pleasure*	Fear
Peyton Manning	Happiness	*Happiness*	Sadness	Contempt	*Joy*
Charles Manson	Anger	Contempt	Anger	Surprise	Satisfaction
Mickey Mantle	Happiness	Surprise	*Pleasure*	Anger	Contempt
Willie Mays	Happiness	*Happiness*	Fear	*Pleasure*	Anger
Joseph McCarthy	Contempt	Anger	Anger	Contempt	Surprise
Paul McCartney	Happiness	*Happiness*	*Pleasure*	Satisfaction	Anger
John McEnroe	Anger	Contempt	Disgust	Sadness	*Joy*
Michael Milken	Fear	Contempt	*Pleasure*	*Joy*	Satisfaction
Joni Mitchell	Happiness	Sadness	Acceptance	Disgust	Anger
Marilyn Monroe	Sadness	Fear	Surprise	Fear	Anger
Joe Montana	*Happiness*	Happiness	*Joy*	Satisfaction	Sadness
Eddie Murphy	*Happiness*	Surprise	Surprise	*Joy*	Sadness
Edward R. Murrow	Happiness	Sadness	Surprise	Fear	Satisfaction
Elon Musk	*Happiness*	Happiness	Disgust	Contempt	Surprise
Cam Newton	Disgust	Anger	Fear	Contempt	*Joy*
Jack Nicholson	Happiness	Anger	Disgust	Surprise	Anger
Jack Nicklaus	Happiness	Contempt	Disgust	Contempt	Surprise
Richard Nixon	Anger	Contempt	Sadness	Anger	Surprise
Greg Norman	*Happiness*	Sadness	Disgust	*Pleasure*	Satisfaction
Barack Obama	Happiness	*Happiness*	Disgust	Contempt	Satisfaction
Jimmy Page	Happiness	*Happiness*	Acceptance	Anger	Fear
Larry Page	Happiness	Surprise	Surprise	Satisfaction	Anger
Ross Perot	Surprise	Happiness	Satisfaction	Fear	Acceptance
Michael Phelps	Happiness	*Happiness*	Surprise	*Joy*	Satisfaction
Brad Pitt	Sadness	Happiness	Satisfaction	Anger	Fear
Robert Plant	Happiness	*Happiness*	Contempt	Acceptance	*Pleasure*
Natalie Portman	Happiness	*Happiness*	Fear	Acceptance	Satisfaction
Elvis Presley	Happiness	Sadness	Disgust	Acceptance	Fear
Prince	Happiness	Surprise	Contempt	Anger	Fear

Name	Highest Voted	2nd Voted	Highest Actual	2nd Actual	Rare
Ronald Reagan	Happiness	Surprise	Fear	Sadness	Acceptance
Robert Redford	Happiness	Surprise	Anger	Satisfaction	Disgust
Mary Lou Retton	*Happiness*	Surprise	*Joy*	*Pleasure*	Anger
Little Richard	*Happiness*	Surprise	Surprise	*Joy*	Satisfaction
Keith Richards	Happiness	Anger	Acceptance	Disgust	Sadness
Jackie Robinson	Sadness	Happiness	Fear	Sadness	Acceptance
Aaron Rodgers	Happiness	Disgust	Contempt	Disgust	*Joy*
Eleanor Roosevelt	Happiness	Sadness	*Pleasure*	Satisfaction	Surprise
Diana Ross	*Happiness*	Happiness	*Pleasure*	Acceptance	Sadness
J. K. Rowling	Happiness	*Happiness*	Contempt	Satisfaction	Fear
Charles Schulz	*Happiness*	Surprise	*Joy*	*Pleasure*	Anger
Amy Schumer	*Happiness*	Surprise	Acceptance	Anger	Fear
Tupac Shakur	Anger	Contempt	Surprise	Acceptance	Satisfaction
O. J. Simpson	Anger	Disgust	Surprise	Fear	Acceptance
Frank Sinatra	Happiness	*Happiness*	Surprise	Fear	Anger
Will Smith	*Happiness*	Happiness	*Pleasure*	*Joy*	Sadness
Edward Snowden	Anger	Contempt	Anger	Acceptance	Disgust
Steven Spielberg	Happiness	Surprise	Acceptance	Surprise	*Joy*
Bruce Springsteen	Happiness	Anger	*Pleasure*	Acceptance	Surprise
Ringo Starr	*Happiness*	Happiness	Satisfaction	*Pleasure*	Anger
Gloria Steinem	Anger	Disgust	Satisfaction	*Joy*	Sadness
Howard Stern	Contempt	Anger	Satisfaction	Anger	Sadness
Jimmy Stewart	*Happiness*	Happiness	Surprise	Fear	Anger
Jon Stewart	Sadness	Anger	Contempt	Surprise	Acceptance
Martha Stewart	Happiness	Contempt	*Pleasure*	Satisfaction	Sadness
Meryl Streep	Happiness	*Happiness*	Acceptance	Anger	*Pleasure*
Taylor Swift	Happiness	*Happiness*	Acceptance	Anger	Surprise
Elizabeth Taylor	Happiness	*Happiness*	Acceptance	Satisfaction	Anger
J. Timberlake	*Happiness*	Happiness	Anger	Contempt	Surprise
Donald Trump	Disgust	Contempt	Sadness	Disgust	Satisfaction
Ivanka Trump	Contempt	Happiness	Disgust	Contempt	Sadness
Lindsey Vonn	Happiness	Surprise	Satisfaction	Contempt	Sadness
George Wallace	Disgust	Anger	Anger	Disgust	Satisfaction
Andy Warhol	Sadness	Fear	Disgust	Sadness	*Pleasure*
Charlie Watts	Happiness	Sadness	Acceptance	Contempt	Sadness
Jack Welch	Happiness	*Happiness*	*Joy*	Anger	Acceptance
Kanye West	Anger	Disgust	Anger	Disgust	Satisfaction
Serena Williams	Happiness	Anger	Disgust	Contempt	*Joy*
Ted Williams	Happiness	Surprise	Disgust	Anger	Fear
Venus Williams	Happiness	Surprise	*Joy*	Sadness	Contempt
Oprah Winfrey	*Happiness*	Happiness	*Joy*	*Pleasure*	Contempt
Kate Winslet	Happiness	*Happiness*	Disgust	Anger	Sadness
Tiger Woods	Sadness	Happiness	Sadness	*Pleasure*	Satisfaction
Bill Wyman	Happiness	Sadness	*Joy*	Anger	Sadness
Mark Zuckerberg	Happiness	*Happiness*	*Joy*	Anger	Fear

Sources & Notes

Besides my benefiting from numerous Wikipedia entries, and drawing on Google Images and YouTube videos for facial coding, other specific sources are cited below.

Introduction

1. Mike Foss, "Peyton Manning Was the No. 1 Pick Because Ryan Leaf Sabotaged the Draft Process," *USA Today*, January 20, 2014, available at http://ftw:usatoday.com/2014/01/how-ryan-leaf-convinced-the-colts-to-draft-peyton-manning; and Kevin Armstrong, "How Ryan Leaf, NFL's Biggest Draft Bust, Turned His Life Around," *The New York Daily News*, May 4, 2016, available at http://www.nydailynews.com/sports/football/ryan-leaf-nfl-biggest-draft-bust-turned-life-article-1.2624679.

2. John Sullivan, ERE Recruiting Conference speech, October 2016. Specifically, Sullivan cited hiring rate failures of 45% for general employees, 40-60% for managers, and 50% for executives. A Heidrick & Struggles 2009 study cites a 40% failure rate for executive hires, lower than the 50-70% rate cited by the Corporate Executive Board. The last two sources are referenced in David Perry's book, *Hiring Greatness: How to Recruit Your Dream Team and Crush the Competition* (New York: Wiley, 2016).

3. Kevin Randall, "Teams Turn to a Face Reader, Looking for That Winning Smile," *The New York Times*, December 26, 2014.

4. Reading faces has two phases, starting with face recognition. The release of the new Apple's iPhoneX with its ability to unlock the screen by "swiping" the user's face belongs to phase one, but is merely a part of something now hitting the big time. Facial recognition software enables everything from tracking church-go'ers attendance, to spotting past shoplifters, and permitting tourists to enter attractions. The Chinese company Megvii already has over 300,000 clients utilizing its face-recognition technology, named Face++, and is the world's first billion-dollar start-up in what *The Economist* has dubbed the "facial-industrial complex." Capturing "faceprints" will become a tidal wave changing business and society at large, whether always welcome or not given the privacy implications. Phase two is emotion recognition, which will also prove transformative. To read more, check out https://www.economist.com/news/leaders/21728617-life-age-facial-recognition-what-machines-can-tell-your-face, and https://www.economist/com/news/business/21728654-chinas-megvii-has-used-government-collected-data-lead-sector-ever-better-and-cheaper.

5. Travis Bradberry and Jean Greaves based their conclusion on results from what they call "the world's most popular EQ test," utilizing a reported online sample of over 500,000 participants to date (San Diego: TalentSmart, 2009).

6. The Voted results reflect an average of 40 votes per celebrity. The Actual results are based on an average of 89 facial muscle movements per celebrity, and typically involved facially coding over 50 photographs per celebrity, with the photos taken during the prime of that person's career. As to the risk of selection bias, I strived to avoid it by working from expressions captured by a variety of photographers on a variety of occasions, working from viable options for facial coding purposes as sequentially available via Google Images, except for when the same look had been captured during the same occasion. Naturally, it's impossible, however, to entirely eliminate selection bias even with those precautions. After all, the photographs are taken in public as opposed to private settings, with the presence of the observer (the photographer and likely others also present) meaning that to some, unverifiable degree a celebrity's branded, public persona may influence everyone involved.

7. Charles Darwin, *The Expressions of the Emotions in Man and Animals*, reprint of original 1872 edition by John Murray (Oxford: Oxford UP, 1998).

8. Perhaps the most striking detail in support of the universality of facial expressions is that even people born blind expresses their feelings the same way that people who can see do. Facial expressions are innate. They're "hard-wired" into the brain, rather than learned. Further evidence is that a child by nine months of age will display all of the seven core emotions covered in this book. In contrast, body language is affected by gender and by culture. For instance, a hand gesture that is just fine in Belgium may get you killed in Sicily. Body language can also be often more easily deployed in manipulative fashion. Case in point: presidential debates are rife with hand gestures that look "faked," as if made on the advice of a debate coach or consultant.

9. Paul Ekman Group, Facial Action Coding System, available at http://www.paulekman.com/product-category/facs/. Other facial coders who have been a resource over the years include: Jeffrey Cohn, a psychology professor at the University of Pittsburgh; and Maggie Pazian, who studied under Ekman's close associate Mark Frank.

10. Paul Ekman, "What Scientists Who Study Emotions Agree About," *Perspectives in Psychological Science* (January 2016). In a survey of 246 quantitative research experts on emotion, 88% agreed that there are universal emotions and 80% agreed that there are universal facial signals for emotions. A contrary voice is Lisa Feldman Barrett, author of *How Emotions Are Made* (Boston: Houghton Mifflin Harcourt, 2017). She considers the FACS model to be overly rigid and simplistic based on assuming it argues for uniform "fingerprints" per emotion. She rightly attacks instances where test subjects around the world were shown a series of photos involved a single posed expression per photo and given a slate of six emotions (minus contempt) to choose from in identifying a correct answer. There is, indeed, as Barrett writes, no single "anger" or "fear" look, as blends of emotions and variations per emotion are commonplace (as illustrated in this book). The odd thing, however, is that FACS documents the "widely varying facial movements" she affirms in her own book. The original 1978 FACS model already listed a variety of complex combinations of facial muscle movements to qualify as showing an emotion, often three or more movements at once. That's a tough standard because in daily life people rarely show that much emotion together. So when I began facial coding after my orientation from Ekman, I soon created a model of allowing each and every facial muscle movement to correspond to one or more emotions as appropriate. That move anticipated the version of FACS scoring Ekman changed to in 2002, thereby further negating Barrett's claims of rigidity.

11. Malcolm Gladwell, *Blink: The Power of Thinking Without Thinking* (New York: Little Brown, 2005).

12. Some examples of wide-ranging media coverage of development-stage versions of automated facial coding software becoming part of the business landscape are available at http://www.wired.com/2016/01/apple-buys-ai-startup-that-reads-emotions-in-faces, https://theintercept.com/2016/08/04/microsoft-pitches-technology-that-can-read-facial-expressions-at-political-rallies/, and http://www.fastcompany.com/3057283/what-happens-when-video-games-can-read-your-face.

13. This conclusion is based on a variety of tests. Some involved facial coding automators asking Sensory Logic to vet their software by sending us video of people whose reactions were coded by them, so my company could then compare their results to ours. In other cases, we've worked from published results and sought to replicate those results by using the same TV spots, but different test subjects, in order to compare

the outcomes. In still other cases, third-party comparison studies on accuracy have been run as competitions by academic institutions or organizations. Finally, a well-credentialed leader in biometrics told me that to date his company relies on the automation software only for the two most obvious emotions: happiness and surprise. They haven't yet found the data sufficiently reliable for the emotions of anger, fear, sadness, disgust, and contempt. Issues with automation can include: not being able to detect quick microexpressions, not distinguishing adequately between smiles and smirks (contempt), and over-reporting the amount of activity on people's faces. The latter problem was dramatized by a U. K. researcher who put a plastic doll in front of a web cam to learn what the software would report. The outcome: supposedly lots of varied facial muscle activity from the doll in response to watching a TV commercial! No wonder the leader of a facial coding automation company admitted on CBS's Evening News in late December 2015 that they "still have a long way to go."

14. Eva G. Krumhuber, Lucas Tamarit, Etienne B. Roesch and Klaus R. Scherer, "FACSGen 2.0 animation software: Generating three-dimensional FACS-valid facial expressions for emotion research," *Emotion*, Vol 12(2), April 2012, 351-363. A study involving four coders FACS-certified (like the author) achieved intercoder reliability levels of 99% for singular facial muscle movements and 81% for combinations of facial muscle movements. Given the greater frequency of singular (versus multiple) movements at a specific moment in time, the net effective accuracy level for high-quality, manual facial coding can exceed 90%.

15. Albert Mahrabian, *Silent Messages* (Belmont, CA: Wadsworth, 1981).

16. Peter Mayle, *Up the Agency: The Funny Business of Advertising* (New York: St. Martin's, 1994).

17. See "The Ability Model of Emotional Intelligence: Principles and Updates," *Emotion Review*, 2016, a collaborative article by John D. Mayer, David R. Caruso, and Peter Salovey. Together, Mayer and Salovey invented the concept of EQ (also known as EI) in 1990, prior to it being popularized by Daniel Goleman in *Emotional Intelligence: Why It Can Matter More than IQ* (New York: Bantam, 1995). Goleman and others have made strong claims for the likely impact of EQ, with extensive research finding a more modest yet solid incremental advantage for those with higher EQ abilities. Besides the many scholarly writings of Mayer and Salovey, readers interested in this topic may also want to explore Daniel Pink's *A Whole New Mind: Why Right-Brainers Will Rule the Future* (New York: Riverhead, 2005).

18. Two examples that build on this model as it relates to specific emotions are Reginald B. Adams, Jr., Nalini Ambady, C. Neil Macrea, and Robert E. Kleck, authors of "Emotional Expressions Forecast Approach-Avoidance Behavior," published online by Springer Science+Business Media in 2006; and Sandeep Gautam, author of "Emotions and Motivations," available at https://www.psychologytoday.com/blog/the-fundamental-four/201205/emotions-and-motivations. As is true of many, even most topics being debated in academia, however, the notion of exactly how many primary emotions there might be, and how best to define them, remain subject to on-going debate. The same can also, in fairness, be said of whether sadness can ever be definitively classified as an approach emotion.

19. In my choosing the 173 celebrities who appear in this book, several filters were used. First, I looked for notable, mostly American born-and-raised celebrities based on their appearing on critics' lists of the greatest achievers in their field, though great commercial success was also a factor at times. Next, I culled the possible options by running my list by several dozen people to learn which options sparked interest

because of a celebrity's personality, biography, or a trend in society he or she has exemplified. Finally, I sought diversity in terms of gender, race, and which era and professional field the celebrities came from.

Anger

1. Geoffrey Wansell, "The Cary Grant That Nobody Knows," available at http://www.carygrant.net/articles/nobody%20knows.html.

2. How myths do hold on, making the negative impact of venting an evergreen news story. Almost 25 years ago this realization got coverage in the Science section of *The New York Times:* Jane Brody, "Venting Anger May Do More Harm than Good," March 8, 1983. NPR, Fox, *Fast Company* and *The Wall Street Journal* have all covered this "news" in the years hence. A recent entry is by Fiona MacDonald, "Sorry, but Venting Online Just Makes You Angrier, Scientists Find," August 15, 2015, available at https://www.sciencealert.com/sorry-but-venting-online-just-makes-you-angrier-scientists-find.

3. This aspect of anger gets touched on by Paul Ekman, *Emotions Revealed* (New York: Henry Holt, 2003). Elevated to hate, it's the focus of an editorial by Anna Fels, "The Point of Hate," *The New York Times,* April 14, 2017.

4. Penelope Gilliatt, "Her Own Best Disputant," *The New Yorker,* December 25, 1978, available at http://www.newyorker.com/magazine/1978/12/25/her-own-best-disputant.

5. Anthony Bozza, "Eminem Blows Up," *Rolling Stone,* November 5, 2009, available at http://www.rollingstone.com/music/news/eminem-blows-up-20091105.

6. Khloe Kardashian, "Khloe: After 10 Years of 'Keeping Up With the Kardashians,' I'm Looking Back," *Glamour,* September 6, 2017, available at https://www.glamour.com/story/khloe-kardashian-looks-back-on-10-years-of-keeping-up-with-the-kardashians.

7. James McWilliams, "John McEnroe and the Sadness of Greatness," *PS Magazine,* September 23, 2013, available at https://psmag.com/john-mcenroe-and-the-sadness-of-greatness-7217ee89a9da#.qnxz05syw.

8. Two separate pieces, four years apart, tell a similar story. The first is Chris Houston, "Blasphemy: The Truth about Michael Jeffrey Jordan," *Bleacher Report,* September 23, 2010, available at http://bleacherreport.com/articles/471875-blasphemy-the-truth-about-michael-jeffrey-jordan/page/2. The second is Jon Wu, "Top 10 Instances of Michael Jordan Being Just Plain Mean," *Bleacher Report,* January 31, 2014, available at http://bleacherreport.com/articles/1943095-top-10-stories-of-michael-jordan-being-the-greatest-jerk-of-all-time/page/2.

9. Anne Helen Petersen, "Scandals of Classic Hollywood: Robert Redford, Golden Boy," *The Hairpin,* May 22, 2013, available at https://www.thehairpin.com/2013/05/scandals-of-classic-hollywood-robert-redford-golden-boy/.

10. James A. Russell may have been the first scholar to apply numerical values, on a limited basis, to some of the facial muscle activities documented by Ekman in FACS. See "Emotions from and into Faces: Resurrecting a Dimensional-Contextual Perspective," in *The Psychology of Facial Expression,* edited by James A. Russell and Jose Miguel Fernandez-Dols (Paris: Cambridge UP, 1997). As best I know, however, I was first to assign numerical values to all of the facial muscle activities in FACS that correspond to emotions, a task that involved some refinements as I began applying the facial coding tool to week-in, week-out research projects for my *Fortune* 500 clients.

11. Joe Klein, *Primary Colors* (New York: Random House, 1996).

12. Hadley Freeman, "Tom Hanks on His Diabetes, Pirates and Rapping with Dan Aykroyd," *The Guardian*, October 10, 2013, available at https://www.theguardian. com/film/2013/oct/10/tom-hanks-diabetes-captain-phillips-interview.

13. Josh Eells, "The Reinvention of Taylor Swift," *Rolling Stone*, September 8, 2014, available at http://www.rollingstone.com/music/features/taylor-swift-1989-cover-story-20140908.

Happiness

1. Malinda Loon, "Back in the Day: Coming Out with Ellen," April 9, 2005, available at http://www/afterellen.com/tv/34682-back-in-the-day-coming-out-with-ellen. For additional perspective, consider Erik Adams, Donna Bowman, Phil Dyess-Nugent, Genevieve Koski, Ryan McGee, David Sims and Todd VanDerWerff, "The Episode That Liberated—Then Destroyed Ellen," August 14, 2013, available at http://www. avclub.com/article/the-episode-that-liberated-then-destroyed-ellen-101551.

2. Daniel McNeil, *The Face: A Natural History* (Boston: Little, Brown, 1998).

3. Marianne LaFrance, *Why Smile: The Science Behind Facial Expressions* (New York: W. W. Norton, 2013).

4. Thomas Hardy, "Neutral Tones" in *Selected Poems* (London: Penguin, 1994).

5. David Michaelis, *Schulz and Peanuts: A Biography* (New York: HarperCollins, 2008).

6. "Mariah Carey Never Played Monroe Piano," available at https://www.msn.com/ en-ph/entertainment/celebrity/mariah-carey-never-played-monroe-piano/ar-BBuWMCM.

7. Mark Lewisohn, *Tune In: The Beatles – All These Years (Vol. 1)*, (New York: Crown, 2013).

8. Laura Jacobs, "Our Lady of the Kitchen," *Vanity Fair*, August 2009, available at http://www.vanityfair.com/culture/2009/08/julia-child200908. Also check out Ruth Reichl, "Julia Child's Recipe for a Thoroughly Modern Marriage," *Smithsonian Magazine*, June 2012, available at http://www.smithsonianmag.com/history/julia-childs-recipe-for-a-thoroughly-modern-marriage-86160745/?no-ist.

9. Nicolaus Mills, "Gloria Steinem's 'A Bunny Tale' – 50 Years Later," *The Guardian*, May 26, 2013, available at https://www.theguardian.com/commentisfree/2013/ may/26/gloria-steinem-bunny-tale-still-relevant-today. Another source is Evelyn Wang at http://www.dazeddigital.com/fashion/article/32834/1/that-time-gloria-steinem-went-undercover-as-a-playboy-bunny.

10. Coverage of Beyonce's childhood and later life includes: http://perezhilton. com/2008-12-30-beyonce-talks-smack-about-the-jacksons#WW9M61Tyu70; http://www.houstonpress.com/music/five-things-we-learned-from-that-beyonce-documentary-on-hbo-6778177; and https://www.forbes.com/forbes/2009/0622/ celebrity-09-jay-z-sasha-fierce-inside-beyonce-empire.html.

11. Kim Kardashian, *Selfish* (New York: Rizzoli, 2015).

12. Vanessa Grigoriadis, "Kim Kardashian: American Woman," *Rolling Stone*, July 27, 2015, available at http://www.rollingstone.com/culture/features/kim-kardashian-american-woman-cover-story-20150727.

13. Jonathan Van Meter, "Amy Schumer Doesn't Care If You Like Her—She's Changing the Game," *Vogue*, June 16, 2016, available at http://www.vogue.com/tag/celebrity/amy-schumer.

14. Jon Mooallem, "Inside the Mind of Steven Spielberg, Hollywood's Big, Friendly Giant," *Wired*, July 2016, available at http://www.wired.com/2016/06/steven-spielberg-the-bfg/.

15. Antonio Garcia Martinez, *Chaos Monkeys* (New York: HarperCollins, 2016).

Sadness

1. Library of Congress, "Forty Years Ago: Nixon's Farewell Remarks to the White House Staff," *Readers Almanac*, (August 7, 2014), available at http://blog.loa.org/2014/08/forty-years-ago-nixon-farewell-remarks.html.

2. Often the eyebrows will rise as part of "speech emphasis." In other words, the person is moving their inner or outer eyebrows to dramatize or illustrate what they're saying. For example, the person might say, "What do you think?" while simultaneously raising their eyebrows. In those cases, it's likely that no emotion is being signaled. Other artifacts that could lead to misinterpreting facial muscle movements include: sucking in one's lips isn't the same as lips pressed together in anger; a movement that comes after people touch their faces isn't likely to signal emotion(s); people stretching their jaws aren't likely to be signaling surprise; and eyes that widen might not signal anything more than a person struggling to stay awake. Getting a baseline, or norm, of a person over time will also help you distinguish between what's likely to be a real sign of emoting versus non-verbal "noise". Therefore, in interviewing a job candidate, as in dating, getting a feel for someone likely benefits from more than a single meeting.

3. Guy Winch, "The Important Difference between Sadness and Depression," *Psychology Today*, October 2015, available at https://www.psychologytoday.com/blog/the-squeaky-wheel/201510/the-important-difference-between-sadness-and-depression.

4. Paul Hendrickson, "Janis Joplin: A Cry Cutting Through Time," *The Washington Post*, May 5, 1998, available at http://www.washingtonpost.com/wp-srv/style/features/joplin.html. Also check out Ellen Willis, "Janis Joplin on Her Own Terms," *Rolling Stone*, November 18, 1976, available at http://www.rollingstone.com/music/news/janis-joplin-on-her-own-terms-9761118.

5. Dan P. McAdams, "The Mind of Donald Trump," *The Atlantic*, June 2016, available at https://www.theatlantic.com/magazine/archive/2016/06/the-mind-of-donald-trump/480771/; and "Harvard Psychologist Explains Trump Is 'Dangerous' Because He's Literally a Narcissistic Psychopath," *Counter Current News*, February 27, 2016, available at https://www.columbiapsychiatry.org/news/harvard-psychologist-explains-trump-dangerous-because-hes-literally-narcissistic-psychopath.

6. Lisa Belkin, "Be a Killer, Be a King: The Education of Donald Trump," Yahoo, July 16, 2016, available at https://www.yahoo.com/news/killer-king-education-donald-trump-000000711.html; also see Maureen Dowd, "The First Porn President," *The New York Times*, March 10, 2018.

7. Joe McGasko, "Remembering Johnny Cash: 10 Things You Might Not Know About Him," *Bio*, September 12, 2013, available at http://www.biography.com/news/johnny-cash-10-interesting-facts.

8. Henry Blodget, "I Asked Jeff Bezos the Tough Questions," *Business Insider,* December 2014, available at http://www.businessinsider.com/amazons-jeff-bezos-on-profits-failure-succession-big-bets-2014-12.

9. Peter Sheridan, "Marlon Brando: A Tormented and Misunderstood Star," *The Telegraph,* June 2014, previously available at http://s.telegraph.co.uk/graphics/projects/marlon-brando/index.html. Also check out Stevan Riley, "Marlon Brando's Secret History," *The Telegraph,* October 16, 2015, available at http://s.telegraph.co.uk/graphics/projects/marlon-brando/index.html.

10. David Fricke, "Kurt Cobain, The Rolling Stone Interview: Success Doesn't Suck," *Rolling Stone,* January 27, 1994, available at http://www.rollingstone.com/music/news/kurt-cobain-the-rolling-stone-interview-19940127.

11. Stephen Galloway, "The Woody Allen Interview (Which He Won't Read)," *The Hollywood Reporter,* May 4, 2016, available at http://www.hollywoodreporter.com/features/woody-allen-interview-he-wont-889678.

12. "Book Reveals Johnny Cash Sick, Grief-Stricken," Associated Press, August 15, 2004, available at http://www.foxnews.com/story/2004/08/15/book-reveals-johnny-cash-sick-grief-stricken.html.

13. Chris Heath, "How Elon Musk Plans on Reinventing the World (and Mars)," *GQ,* December 12, 2015, available at http://www.gq,com/story/elon-musk-mars-spacex-texla-interview.

Flash Portraits

1. Larry Tye, "Reintroducing Bobby Kennedy and His Legacy," *Prospect,* June 21, 2016, available at http://prospect.org/article/reintroducing-bobby-kennedy-and-his-legacy.

2. "Watching Serena and Venus Williams' Dad Predict the Outcome of His Daughters' Great Tennis Rivalry in This 1992 Clip," *The Week,* available at http://theweek.com/speedreads/576003/watch-serena-venus-williams-dad-predict-outcome-daughters-great-tennis-rivalry-1992-clip.

3. Michael Jackson, *Moonwalk* (New York: Doubleday: 1988).

4. Iona Kirby, "Brad Pitt Reveals He Was 'Wasting' His Life Away while Married to Jennifer Aniston," *The Daily Mail,* May 21, 2013, available at http://www.dailymail.co.uk/tvshowbiz/article-2328477/Brad-Pitt-reveals-wasting-life-away-married-Jennifer-Aniston.html.

5. "Hillary Clinton's Strengths and Anger in White House Revealed" by Alex Seitz-Wald, Nov. 26, 2014, see http://www.msnbc.com/msnbc/hillary-clintons-strengths-and-anger-white-house-revealed. Also discussed in George Stephanopoulos's autobiography, *All Too Human: A Political Education* (Boston: Little, Brown, 1999).

6. Hannah Al-Othman, "Trump Jokes He Has 'Sex' in Common with Daughter Ivanka in Bizarre Wendy Williams Interview," *The Daily Mail,* October 25, 2016, available at http://www.dailymail.co/uk/news/article-3870754/the-thing-common-sex-bizarre-interview-Donald-Ivanka-Trump-resurfaces-three-years-later.html.

7. "Beyonce: Marriage to Jay-Z 'A Power Struggle,'" *Access Hollywood,* December 30, 2008, available at https://www.accesshollywood.com/articles/beyonce-marriage-to-jay-z-a-power-struggle-66881/.

Contempt

1. Maureen Orth, "Scientology: What Katie Didn't Know," *Vanity Fair,* October 2012, available at http://www.vanityfair.com/hollywood/2012/10/katie-holmes-divorce-scientology.

2. Jade Watkins, "Matt Lauer Admits Cold War Period After Tom Cruise Called Him Glib in Infamous Interview," *The Daily Mail,* June 21, 2013, available at http://www.dailymail.co.uk/tvshowbiz/article-2345978/Matt-Lauer-admits-cold-war-period-Tom-Cruise-called-glib-infamous-interview-reveals-actor-wanted-rant-removed-from-air.

3. A. H. Fischer and I. J. Roseman, "Beat Them or Ban Them: The Characteristics and Social Functions of Anger and Contempt," *Journal of Personality & Social Psychology,* 93, 2007.

4. Malcolm Gladwell, *Op. Cit.*

5. Tina Brown, "Diana's Final Heartbreak," *Vanity Fair,* July 2007, available at http://www.vanityfair.com/news/2007/07/diana200707.

6. James Hansen, "The Truth About Neil Armstrong," *Space,* August 23, 2013, available at http://www.space.com/22510-neil-armstrong-astronaut-icon-remembered.html.

7. Coverage of Hillary Clinton's post-defeat demeanor includes, perhaps most prominently, David Remnick's piece at https://www.newyorker.com/magazine/2017/09/25/hillary-clinton-looks-back-in-anger. Also check out: Peggy Noonan at http://www.peggynoonan.com/hillary-lacks-remorse-of-conscience/. Among Clinton's 2008 campaign coverage is "The Tears Over Coffee That Turned Round Poll" at https://www.theguardian.com/world/2008/jan/10/hillaryclinton.uselections20082. Relevant conference appearance highlights include: https://www.youtube.com/watch?v=pXE2qEfhIDY for the interview with CNN's Christiana Amanpour at the 2017 Women for Women International luncheon; and https://www.youtube.com/watch?v=KgdJlzuaJ6k for Clinton being interviewed at the Code 2017 conference.

8. Jason Heller, "12 Wildest Prince Moments," *Rolling Stone,* April 22, 2016, available at http://www.rollingstone.com/music/lists/12-wildest-prince-moments-20160422.

9. Steve Kettmann, "The World's Richest Crybaby: How Bill Gates' Arrogance Led to His Decline and Fall," *SF Gate,* February 11, 2001, available at http://www.sfgate/com/books/article/the-World's-Richest-Crybaby-How-Bill-Gates-2953310.php.

10. Simon Davis, "Bill Gates Arrogant as Napoleon, Says Judge," *The Telegraph,* January 9, 2001, available at http://www.telegraph.co.uk/news/worldnews/1314005/Bill-Gates-arrogant-as-Napoleon-says-judge.html.

11. Ian Parker, "Mugglemarch: J. K. Rowling Writes a Realistic Novel for Adults," *The New Yorker,* October 1, 2012, available at http://www.newyorker.com/magazine/2012/10/01/mugglemarch.

12. Ian Parker, *Op. Cit.*

13. Scott Wilson, "Obama, the Loner President," *The Washington Post,* October 7, 2011, available at https://www.washingtonpost.com/opinions/obama-the-loner-president/2011/10/03/gIQAHFcSTL_story.html?utm_term=.e61327fcf1d7.

14. Maureen Dowd, *The Year of Voting Dangerously: The Derangement of American Politics* (New York: Hatchette, 2016). To learn the depth of the intransigent, hard-ball manuevering Obama faced, check out Jane Mayer's *Dark Money: The Hidden History of the Billionaires Behind the Rise of the Radical Right* (New York:Doubleday, 2016).

15. "Oral History: Prince's Life, as Told by the People Who Knew Him Best," *The Minneapolis Star-Tribune*, April 29, 2016, available at http://www.startribune.com/the-life-of-prince-as-told-by-the-people-who-knew-him/376586581/#1.

16. Roger Ebert, "Hugh Hefner Has Been Good for Us," October 24, 2010, available at http://www.rogerebert.com/rogers-journal/hugh-hefner-has-been-good-for-us. For unsavory details related to the demise of Hefner's estate, look up Brooks Barnes's story, "Behind Glamour of the Playboy Mansion Lurked a Sometimes Ugly Reality," *The New York Times*, September 29, 2017, B6.

17. Mike Larkin, "Tiger Woods Put Her Off Marriage! Champion Skier Lindsey Vonn Admits Troubled Love Life Made Her Wary of Getting Wed on Running Wild," *The Daily Mail*, September 6, 2016, available at http://www.dailymail.co.uk/tvshowbiz/article-3775530/Lindsey-Vonn-reveals-Tiger-Woods-marriage-Running-Wild-Bear-Grylls.html.

18. John Fricke, *Judy: A Legendary Film Career* (New York: Running Press, 2011).

Disgust

1. Mandy Van Deven, "The Science Behind Disgust," *Salon*, July 24, 2011, available at http://www.salon.com/2011/07/24/disgust_interview/.

2. "Elvis Presley Bio," *Rolling Stone*, available at http://www.rollingstone.com/music/artists/elvis-presley/biography.

3. Katherine Q. Seelye and Jeff Zelemy, "On the Defensive, Obama Calls His Words Ill-Chosen," *The New York Times*, April 13, 2008, available at http://www.nytimes.com/2008/04/13/us/politics/13campaign.html.

4. Marc Berman, "Ayesha Curry, Klay Thompson Pile on LeBron: He's a Crybaby," *The New York Post*, June 12, 2016, available at https://nypost.com/2016/06/12/ayesha-curry-klay-thompson-pile-on-lebron-hes-a-crybaby/.

5. Benjamin Genocchio, "When 'Delinquents Infiltrated Art," *The New York Times*, May 11, 2003.

6. Anthony DeCurtis, "Whitney Houston Opens Up About Her Marriage, Fame," *Rolling Stone*, June 10, 1993, available at http://www.rollingstone.com/music/news/whitney-houston-opens-up-about-her-marriage-the-pressures-of-fame-and-more-20120212.

7. Mark Seal, "Inside Whitney Houston's Final Days—And Her Troubled Relationships," *Vanity Fair*, May 3, 2012, available at https://www.vanityfair.com/culture/2012/05/whitney-houston-final-days-mark-seal.

8. Erick Fernandez, "15 Years Ago, Roger Clemens Infamously Tossed a Bat Toward Mike Piazza," *The Huffington Post*, October 22, 2015, available at http://www.huffingtonpost.com/entry/roger-clemens-throws-bat-mike-piazza_us_562828a4e4b02f6a900f9486.

9. Claudia Rankine, "The Meaning of Serena Williams," *The New York Times*, August 25, 2015, available at https://www.nytimes.com/2015/08/30/magazine/the-meaning-of-serena-williams.html.

10. A long-standing rumor is that Elvis Presley supposedly said, "The only thing Negroes can do for me is buy my records and shine my shoes." It's claimed Presley said so at a concert in Boston before he'd ever visited that city, and the quote was later explicitly disavowed by Presley himself. There's likewise plenty of evidence of Presley's support of black culture based, in part, on his friendships with James Brown, Ike Turner, B. B. King, Cissy Houston, and Muhammad Ali, among others. That said, Presley and the topic of white musicians appropriating African-American songs is a long-standing, complex issue more fully explored in sources like https://www.thedailybeast.com/the-truth-about-elvis-and-the-history-of-racism-in-rock; and http://www.newsweek.com/elvis-presley-40-years-later-was-king-rock-n-roll-guilty-appropriating-black-651911.

11. Phil Picardi, "On This Day in 1954, Elvis Is Heard on the Radio for the First Time," Minnesota Public Radio, July 8, 2014.

12. Grant Brisbee, "MLB Umpires and the Classification of Strike-Three Calls," *SB Nation*, July 9, 2012, available at http://www.sbnation.com/2012/7/9/3142348/mlb-umpire-strike-three-calls.

13. Krista Smith, "Isn't She Deneuvely?" *Vanity Fair*, December 2008, available at http://www.vanityfair.com/news/2008/12/winslet200812.

14. Sheila Weller, "Jimi Hendrix: 'I Don't Want to Be a Clown Anymore,'" *Rolling Stone,* November 15, 1969, available at http://www.rollingstone.com/music/news/jimi-hendrix-i-dont-want-to-be-a-clown-anymore-19691115.

15. Lili Anolik, "How O. J. Simpson Killed Popular Culture," *Vanity Fair*, June 2014, available at https://www.vanityfair.com/style/society/2014/06/oj-simpson-trial-reality-tv-pop-culture.

16. Amy Reyes, "Kanye West's Five Weirdest (and Greatest) Stories of 2016 (So Far)," *Miami,* September 14, 2016, available at http://www.miami.com/miami-news/kanye-wests-five-weirdest-and-greatest-stories-of-2016-so-far-22169/.

17. Anne Helen Petersen, "Scandals of Classic Hollywood: Elizabeth Taylor, Black Widow," *The Hairpin*, July 25, 2011, available at https://www.thehairpin.com/2011/07/scandals-of-classic-hollywood-elizabeth-taylor-black-widow/.

Flash Portraits

1. Ashleyvr, "Oprah Winfrey vs. Ellen Degeneres," available at https://oprahwinfrey12.wordpress.com2012/12/10/oprah-winfrey-vs-ellen-degeneres.

2. Buzz Bissinger, "Caitlyn Jenner: The Full Story," *Vanity Fair,* July 2015, available at http://www.vanityfair.com/hollywood/2015/06/caitlyn-jenner-bruce-cover-annie-leibovitz.

3. Rob Hoerburger, "Long Live Aretha, the Queen of Soul," *The New York Times Magazine,* July 8, 2011, available at http://www.nytimes.com/2011/07/10/magazine/long-live-aretha-the-queen-of-soul.html.

4. Matt Weinberger, "The Strange Love-Hate Relationship between Bill Gates and Steve Jobs," *Business Insider*, March 10, 2016, available at http://www.businessinsider.com/the-bill-gates-steve-jobs-feud-frenemies-2016-3/#gates-wasnt-particularly-impressed-with-what-he-saw-as-a-limited-platform.

5. Ed Vulliamy, "Jim Hendrix: 'You Never Told Me He Was That Good,'" *The Guardian*, August 7, 2010, available at https://theguardian.com/music/2010/august/08/jimi-hendrix-40th-anniversary-death.

6. Rich Cohen, "Inside Mick Jagger and Keith Richard's Five-Decade Bromance," *Vanity Fair,* April 2016, available at http://www.vanityfair.com/culture/2016/03/mick-jagger-keith-richards-rich-cohen.

7. Allen Barra, "Hank Aaron and Willie Mays: New Revelations on Just How Much They Hated Each Other," *The Village Voice,* May 4, 2010, available at https://www.villagevoice.com/2010/05/04/hank-aaron-and-willie-mays-new-revelations-on-just-how-much-they-hated-each-other/.

8. Rob Jones, "Who Is the Next Bob Dylan?: 10 Songwriters Once Voted Most Likely," January 3, 2013, The Delete Bin, available at https://thedeletebin.com/2013/01/03/who-is-the-next-bob-dylan-10-songwriters-once-voted-most-likely/.

Surprise

1. Kate Aurthur, "18 Moments That Led to Bill Cosby's Stunning Downfall," *Buzzfeed,* November 21, 2014, available at https://www.buzzfeed.com/kateaurthur/18-moments-that-led-to-bill-cosbys-stunning-downfall?utm_term=.pilknLGNE#.kb74NkVDz.

2. John Williams asks authors five questions in his columns, in this case of Mario Livio, the author of *Why: What Makes Us Curious.* See https://www.nytimes.com/2017/07/16/books/mario-livio-why-what-makes-us-curious.html for further details.

3. Daniel Kahneman, *Thinking, Fast and Slow* (New York: Farrar, Straus and Giroux, 2011).

4. Gay Talese, "Frank Sinatra Has a Cold," *Esquire,* April 1966, available at http://www.esquire.com/news-politics/a638/frank-sinatra-has-a-cold-talese/.

5. Sarah Moughty, "20 Years After HIV Announcement, Magic Johnson Emphasizes: 'I Am Not Cured,'" *PBS,* November 7, 2011, available at https://www.pbs.org/wgbh/frontline/article/20-years-after-hiv-announcement-magic-johnson-emphasizes-i-am-not-cured/.

6. Maureen Dowd, "'My Life So Far': The Roles of a Lifetime," *The New York Times,* April 24, 2005, available at http://www.nytimes.com/2005/04/24/books/review/my-life-so-far-the-roles-of-a-lifetime.html.

7. Sarah Bibel, "6 Lesser-Known Facts about Audrey Hepburn," *Bio,* May 3, 2015, available at http://www.biography.com/news/audrey-hepburn-facts-biography.

8. Gay Talese, *Op. Cit.*

9. Mikel Gilmore, "How Muhammad Ali Conquered Fear and Changed the World," *Men's Journal,* June 2016, available at https://www.mensjournal.com/featureshow-muhammad-ali-conquered-fear-and-changed-the-world-20130205.

10. Steve Tobak, "Alphabet CEO Larry Page Needs Adult Supervision," Fox Business, August 15, 2016, available at http://www.foxbusiness.com/features/2016/08/15/alphabet-ceo-larry-page-needs-adult-supervision.html.

11. Justin Bariso, "Adele Turning Down the Super Bowl Teaches All of Us a Major Lesson," *Inc.,* August 6, 2016, available at https://www.inc.com/justin-bariso/adele-turning-down-the-super-bowl-teaches-all-of-us-a-major-lesson.html.

12. Brian Hiatt, "Adele: Inside Her Private Life and Triumphant Return," *Rolling Stone,* November 3, 2015, available at http://www.rollingstone.com/music/news/adele-inside-her-private-life-and-triumphant-return-20151103.

Fear

1. Allysia Finley, "What Bill and Hillary Could Tell Tom Brady," *Wall Street Journal*, May 8, 2015, available at https://www.wsj.com/articles/what-bill-and-hillary-could-tell-tom-brady-1431040303. To view Brady's deflategate press conference, check out https://www.youtube.com/watch?v=lhslsyH3PlY.

2. Alexander Todorov, *Face Value: The Irresistible Influence of First Impressions* (Princeton, NJ: Princeton UP, 2017). The fusiform face area (FFA), the amygdala, and the hippocampus (involved in memory functions) are all key components active in the brain's neural systems in order to help us understand others.

3. Kasia and Patryk Wezowski, *The Micro Expressions Book for Business* (Belgium: New Vision, 2012).

4. Jonathan Van Meter, "Jennifer Aniston: Prime Time," *Vogue*, December 1, 2008, available at https://www.vogue.com/article/jennifer-aniston-prime-time.

5. Stephen Galloway, "Jennifer Aniston Reveals Struggles with Dyslexia, Anger; Shrugs Off Oscar Snub," *The Hollywood Reporter*, January 21, 2015, available at http://www.hollywoodreporter.com/news/jennifer-aniston-reveals-struggles-dyslexia-764854.

6. J. Randy Taraborrelli, "Joe DiMaggio Wanted Marilyn Monroe to Be His Demure Housewife, So When She Posed for This Picture He Beat Her Up," *The Daily Mail*, September 1, 2009, available at http://www.dailymail.co/uk/femail/article-1210384/Joe-DiMaggio-wanted-Marilyn-Monroe-demure-housewife-posed-picture-beat-up.html.

7. Sandra McKee, "Gretzky's Goal: Overcoming Fear," *The Baltimore Sun*, March 9, 1994, available at http://articles.baltimoresun.com/1994-03-09/sports/1994068073_1_fear-star-wayne-gretzky-gretzky-scored.

8. Wayne Drehs, "Michael Phelps' Final Turn," *ESPN*, July 18, 2016, available at http://www.espn.com/espn/feature/story/_/id/16425548/michael-phelps-prepares-life-2016-rio-olympics.

9. Few celebrities have publicly admitted to self-doubt more than Portman. Among the sources to consider: Chris Heath, "The Private Life of Natalie Portman," *Rolling Stone*, June 20, 2002, available at http://www.rollingstone.com/culture/news/the-private-life-of-natalie-portman-rolling-stones-2002-cover-story-20110120; Gill Pringle, "Natalie Portman – More Than a Woman," *The Independent*, February 28, 2008, available at http://www.independent.co.uk/arts-entertainment/films/features/natalie-portman-more-than-a-woman-789103.html; and Christina Pazzanese, "Portman: I, Too, Battled Self-Doubt," *The Harvard Gazette*, May 27, 2015, available at https://news.harvard.edu/gazette/story/2015/05/portman-i-too-battled-self-doubt/.

10. Arthur Miller, *Timebends: A Life* (New York: Grove, 2013).

11. Sara Boboltz, "Here's What You Might Not Remember About O. J. Simpson's Police Chase," *The Huffington Post*, February 9, 2016, available at http://www.huffingtonpost.com/entry/american-crime-story-oj-simpson-bronco-chase_us_56b8f737e4b01d80b2475fc7.

12. Chris Spargo, "OJ Simpson's Agent Claims He Admitted to Stabbing Nicole Brown to Death," *The Daily Mail*, June 18, 2016, available at http://www.dailymail.co.uk/news/article-3648762/OJ-Simpson-s-agent-claims-football-star-chilling-murder-confession-admitted-stabbing-Nicole-Brown-death.html.

13. Twin sources here consist of: Julie Miller, "Jane Fonda Is 'So Jealous' of Jennifer Lawrence and Amy Schumer's Friendship," *Vanity Fair*, February 2, 2016, available at http://www.vanityfair.com/hollywood/2016/02/jane-fonda-jennifer-lawrence; and Maureen Dowd, "'My Life So Far': The Roles of a Lifetime," *Op. Cit.*

14. Jon Meachem, "Nostalgia for the Grace of George H. W. Bush," *The New York Times*, October 15, 2016, available at https://www.nytimes.com/2016/10/16/opinion/nostalgia-for-the-grace-of-george-hw-bush.html.

15. Matt Weinberger, "The Rise of Larry Ellison, the Jet-Setting Billionaire Founder of Oracle," *Business Insider*, January 16, 2017, available at http://www.businessinsider.com/rise-of-oracle-founder-larry-ellison-2017-1.

16. Peter King, "Tom Brady Tells the Story of the Super Bowl 51 Comeback," *Sports Illustrated*, February 13, 2017, available at https://www.si.com/mmqb/2017/02/13/tom-brady-montana-super-bowl-51-nfl-patriots-peter-king.

17. Brooks Barnes, "Following Her Fears to Greater Heights," *The New York Times*, September 6, 2013, available at http://ww.nytimes.com/2013/09/08/movies/sandra-bullock-may-be-hollywoods-gutsiest-a-list-actress.html?pagewanted+all&_r=0.

18. Peggy Noonan, "Ronald Reagan," *PBS*, available at https://www.pbs.org/newshour/spc/character/essays/reagan.html.

19. Mikal Gilmore. *Op. Cit.*

Epilogue

1. Yudhijit Bhattacharjee, "Why We Lie," *National Geographic,* June 2017.

2. Timothy Wilson, *Strangers to Ourselves: Discovering the Adaptive Unconscious* (Cambridge, MA: Belknap Press, 2002).

3. David Livingstone Smith, *Why We Lie: The Evolutionary Roots of Deception and the Unconscious Mind* (New York: St. Martin's Griffin, 2004).

4. Yudhijit Bhattacharjee, *Op. Cit.*

5. The video clip, "President Dwight Eisenhower speaks about the U-2 Spy Trials at Moscow Trade Union," is available at https://www.youtube.com/watch?v=ZIddDfbBuBc. Not only did Eisenhower tell his secretary, "I would like to resign" in response to the scandal, he also felt that his U-2 "lie was one of the deepest regrets of his presidency." The incident appears in Sheryl Gay Stolberg's article, "Many Politicians Lie, but Trump Has Elevated the Art of Fabrication," *The New York Times*, August 7, 2017.

6. Lying is discussed in depth in Paul Ekman's book, *Telling Lies: Clues to Deceit in the Marketplace, Politics, and Marriage* (New York: Norton, 1992).

7. Zara Ambadar, Jeffrey Cohn, and Lawrence Ian Read, "All Smiles are Not Created Equal: Morphology and Timing of Smiles Perceived as Amused, Polite, and Embarrassed/Nervous," *Journal of Nonverbal Behavior,* 2008.

8. Regarding 2012, look to stories like the one published in *USA Today* on October 11th, "Biden's Frequent Smiles During Debate Ignite Twitter." In 2016, you can view Biden's remarks at https://www.youtube.com/watch?v=Ueq-hvKLUDM.

9. See "Rachel Dolezal Breaks Her Silence: 'I Identify As Black' / Today" at https://www.today.com/news/rachel-dolezal-speaks-today-show-matt-lauer-after-naacp-resignation-t26371.

10. See "President Reagan's Television Address on the Iran-Contra Affair – 1987" at https://www.youtube.com/watch?v=iOlVfoBouus. Despite Oliver North saying "President Reagan didn't always know what he knew," Reagan almost surely knew that he had explicitly directed White House officials not to tell the U.S. Congress about the Israelis serving as middlemen in the selling of arms to Iran. Among the coverage, check out "North Says Reagan Knew of Iran Ideal" at http:www.nytimes.com/1991/10/20/us/north-says-reagan-knew-of-iran-deal.html?pagewanted=all;
    and "How the Reagan White House Bungled Its Response to Iran-Contra Revelations" at https://www.thedailybeast.com/how-the-reagan-white-house-bungled-its-response-to-iran-contra-revelations.

11. Paul Ekman, *Telling Lies, Op. Cit.*

12. Despite the erroneous assumption that moments of extreme emoting should be readily associated with a single emotion, Alexander Todorov, *Op. Cit.*, offers many valid examples of mistakes made based on first impressions of others. Physiognomy means: "a person's facial features or expression, especially when regarded as indicative of character or ethnic origin." It's similar in intent to phrenology ("the detailed study of the shape and size of the cranium as a supposed indication of character and mental ability"). Both pseudo-scientific approaches invite dubious judgments about an individual's mental and moral qualities. In reality, no physical attribute involving one's head or face makes it possible to reliably assess, for instance, an individual's trustworthiness. Otherwise, definitive clues to lying would exist.

Celebrity Index

Page numbers pertain to a celebrity in the 173-celebrity sample getting cited. Famous people not in the sample aren't listed here.

Acknowledgments

"Books are never finished, they are merely abandoned" quipped Oscar Wilde. I've been lucky to have many people who kept me from wrapping up *Famous Faces Decoded* prematurely. First and foremost, gratitude is due to my wife, Karen Bernthal, for her considerable editorial input and also bringing her artistic talents to bear on all of the book's many graphic elements. I could not have created this book without her. Next up is Joe Bockman, to whom I'm grateful for compiling the statistics that helped shape this book.

Holly Buchanan and Anne Jones both read the manuscript in full and offered good, deft suggestions for improvement. Besides my father and in-laws, others who helped out include: Tim Dennis, Paul Feroe, Steve Goodyear, Gary Jader, Dave Kenney, Kristin Kladstrup, Jerry Lee, Kathryn and Scott Mathews Christie & Mark McLean, Peter Narum, Shirley Ochi-Watson, Anita and David Perry, Emmanuel Probst, Nelson and Patty Rhodus, Margaret Radke, Kathy Seamon, Becky Seavey, Joel Stern, Natalie Sudman, Dan Wallace, and John Weddle. Taylor Atkinson and Ron Standord kindly proofread the book's penultimate draft.

Earlier in the process, many people, far too numerous to name here, helped to provide suggestions on which celebrities to facially code. Hundreds of other people then participated in voting on the celebrities' most distinctive emotions. Lauren DeBueriis and Laura Dragne were particularly helpful in securing the voting input. To one and all, my heartfelt appreciation!

About the Author

Dan Hill, Ph.D., is the founder and president of Sensory Logic, Inc., which pioneered the use of facial coding in business beginning in 1998. As an expert facial coder, Dan is the recipient of seven U.S. patents related to advanced methods for the scoring and analysis of facial coding data. He's also a certified Facial Action Coding System (FACS) practitioner. Dan has done consulting work for over half of the world's top 100 B2C companies. Among his five previous books is *Emotionomics*, chosen by *Advertising Age* as one of the top 10 must-read books of 2009, which featured a foreword by Sam Simon, co-creator of *The Simpsons* in its second edition.

Dan's TV appearances have ranged from ABC's "Good Morning America," Al Jazeera, Bloomberg TV, CNBC, CNN, ESPN, Fox, MSNBC, NBC's "The Today Show," and PBS, to The Tennis Channel. For radio, Dan has been interviewed by the BBC and NPR's "Marketplace". Print and digital coverage of Dan's work has included: *Admap, Advertising Age, Adweek, Allure, Entrepreneur, Fast Company, The Financial Times, Forbes China, Inc., Kiplinger's, The Los Angeles Times, The New York Times, Politico, Time, USA Today,* and *Wall Street Journal,* in addition to his having been a columnist for Reuters. His essays were noted with commendation in the 1989, 1991 and 1994 editions of *The Best American Essays.*

Since his education at St. Olaf College, Oxford University, Brown University, and Rutgers University, Dan has given speeches and led workshops in over 20 countries. Along with his wife, Karen Bernthal, he lives in St. Paul, Minnesota and Palm Desert, California.

DECODING FACES:
APPLICATIONS IN YOUR LIFE

In this supplement to *Famous Faces Decoded: A Guidebook for Reading Others*, the focus shifts from examples involving the lives of celebrities to situations you encounter in your daily life. For every core facial coding emotion, *Decoding Faces* will tell you how the expressions covered in *Famous Faces Decoded* apply at work, in dating, marriage, or handling your kids. Packed with advice while providing a helpful checklist of ways to practice reading others, you can use this book as a compass in navigating the emotional aspects of interpersonal dynamics.

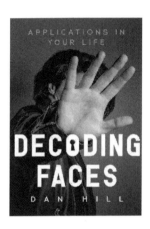

"Faces of the Week"

I publish short blogs on newsworthy, current events that catch my eye and heart. Some are snarky, some merely ironic; others aim to be compassionate regarding celebrities and other people in the headlines whose stories have an emotional dimension to them. Each blog includes at least one photograph, facially coded, so that you can keep refining your ability to read the emotions of others.

To follow my blog go to

@EmotionsWizard.com

"WHO ARE YOU?"

bellows the Wizard of Oz when Dorothy and
her companions reach the Emerald City.

I ask the same question.

Famous Faces Decoded is about building better rapport with others. So it's natural to invite you, my reader, to raise questions on topics you're curious about. For a dialogue to happen, I've created a place for your input on my web site. Go to https://SensoryLogic.com/input and while I can't promise to reply to every inquiry, some responses will be part of my quarterly enewsletter about interesting books and events involving emotional intelligence (EQ).

Here's a Free Offer.

Join the other people WHO have already subscribed to my enewsletter at www.SensoryLogic.com, and in return you'll receive, for free, the 68-page downloadable companion ebook:

DECODING FACES:
APPLICATIONS IN YOUR LIFE

Once you have subscribed, go to

https://SensoryLogic.com/ebookoffer

Others you tell are eligible, too!

EMOTIONOMICS WINNING HEARTS AND MINDS

DAN HILL

There are two currencies in business: money and feelings. The book that first brought behavioral economics into business on an actionable basis is back in its original, image-rich, color format on the 10th anniversary of its release. In this new edition, the fully restored content covers the role of emotions in both the marketplace and workplace, from branding, offer design, packaging, usability, advertising, sales, and the customer shopping experience, to leadership and employee management.

Thought leaders who have endorsed Dan's business books include: Dan Ariely, Scott Bedbury, Jeffrey Gitomer, Martin Lindstrom, Howard Moskowitz, B. Joseph Pine II, Faith Popcorn, Al Ries, and Kevin Roberts.

Available on Amazon.

"Get ready for a wild ride. In this fast-moving survey of the state of the art, Dan Hill takes you from facial expressions to traffic signs. You'll discover something cool on every page."
—Seth Godin

"*Emotionomics* is a truly unique read. Mr. Hill's cutting edge applications of sensory, emotional, and rational research are a must for today's business environment."
—Daniel H. Pink

"This is not your dry business tome. Dan's written a modern book for a modern reader—well designed, great content, fascinating subject. It works on your bookshelf or your coffee table."
—Paco Underhill

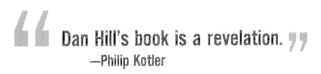

Dan Hill's book is a revelation.
—Philip Kotler

Book Dan as your next speaker

Dan delivers fresh, incisive keynotes on emotional intelligence related to leadership, sales, customer-centric business strategies, and employee engagement. *Famous Faces Decoded* can also come to life via entertaining, personality-driven presentations regarding newsworthy current affairs involving politics, sports, Hollywood, and more. Topics that blend business and fun are his forté and can be customized to fit your needs.

Praise for speeches and workshops

"I cannot remember the last time I enjoyed a presentation so much, Dan. Thank you. We have had great feedback from everyone in the room (even the guys running the sound and lights told me they were gripped from start to finish!). But as well as educating and entertaining us, you also made a cast-iron case for the VALUE of empathy and emotional insight. I am going to rush out and get myself a copy of *Emotionomics*! Thank you so much."

—Matthew Banks, Oracle

"Great job today—I don't remember that group [our executive board] ever applauding after a presentation. The meeting was an A+."

—Vice President, Life Insurance Marketing Research Association (LIMRA)

"I thought you would be interested to have feedback from delegates on your session. They rated the content at 93% and your style at 99%—obviously making you the star of the show!"

—Deborah Parkes, Executive Director, Future Foundation (U. K.)

"What a great event this morning—I LOVE, LOVE, LOVE the topic and will be purchasing Dan's books to share with my staff here. I could have listened to Dan's subject matter all day—fascinating stuff."

—Audrey Isaac, Director, American Museum of Natural History (NYC)

"What a fun lecture last night! The students *loved* it. They found what you had to say so helpful and useful. You say it better, funnier, and with more credibility than I could, and for that I am truly grateful."

—Kathleen Vohs, Carlson School of Management (University of Minnesota)

For specifics, go to:

www.**sensorylogic**.com
click on **Speaking**

Book Club Discussion Questions

Big Picture

1. What are this book's main ideas, messages, and themes?

2. What new things did you learn?

3. Why does this book matter? What was the author's purpose?

4. What preconceptions were challenged, including by gender?

5. What was the most surprising or intriguing aspect of this book?

Specific Celebrities

1. What Top 10 list result surprised you the most/least?

2. Which celebrity flash-portrait comparison is most illuminating?

3. Which of the 28 forms of emotion most got your attention?

4. What was your favorite celebrity story in this book?

5. Which example of a parent's influence struck you the most?

6. Which celebrity example did you learn the most from?

7. Which celebrities did you come away liking more/less than before?

8. Which if any celebrities in this book remain a mystery to you?

Personally

1. What was your favorite quote or passage?

2. Did this book change your perspective about anything?

3. How does this book relate to your life experiences?

4. What will you be able to do differently after reading this book?

5. Who are other celebrities you would like to learn about?

6. If you could ask the author one question, what would it be?

Made in the USA
Middletown, DE
26 September 2018